Reflections on the Meaning of Mental Integrity

Reflections on the Meaning of Mental Integrity

Recovery from Serious Mental Illness

MARCIA A. MURPHY

RESOURCE *Publications* · Eugene, Oregon

REFLECTIONS ON THE MEANING OF MENTAL INTEGRITY
Recovery from Serious Mental Illness

Resource Publications
An Imprint of Wipf and Stock Publishers
199 W. 8th Ave., Suite 3
Eugene, OR 97401

www.wipfandstock.com

PAPERBACK ISBN: 978-1-6667-0889-9
HARDCOVER ISBN: 978-1-6667-0890-5
EBOOK ISBN: 978-1-6667-0891-2

11/22/21

With gratitude to Cecilia M. Redmond-Norris, MD

For I know the plans I have for you, declares the Lord,
plans for welfare and not for evil, to give you a future and a hope.

JEREMIAH 29:11 (ESV)

Contents

Acknowledgments

I AM GRATEFUL FOR all the librarians in my life for the assistance they give in supporting my research. Thank you.

I am also grateful for the many baristas that have brightened my mornings with a hot cup of java.

And since I am a person who has never owned a vehicle, I want to thank the numerous city transit bus drivers who take me from one place to another so I can do my writing. They are truly heroes, going out in all kinds of weather—sub-zero, with ice covered roads, as well as sweltering heat—who also tolerate the social conditions that come with working with an unpredictable public; and who say consistently, with real warmth as I disembark from the bus: *Enjoy your day!*

Author's Note

In order to protect the privacy of individuals involved some names, characteristics, and locations have been altered. The exceptions are names of prominent figures and institutions which are known to the public.

Introduction

I'm running for my life. My feet, heavy as blocks of iron, I strain to raise them up and place them back in front again one after the other. Fleeing in the dark of night away from my deadly pursuer, I turn to look back over my shoulder and then keep running, running, my lungs burning. Down the cavernous streets of Manhattan, turning one way, then another, gray high-rise buildings on every side, dodging blurring, faceless beings everywhere which ignore me as I try to escape. He can't keep up and soon disappears from sight, but I keep running, running, running. Then slowly, finally out of breath with my side in excruciating pain, I collapse.

❖ ❖ ❖

I needed to leave the violence in my home in the Midwest, so at eighteen years of age I was easy prey for pseudoreligious cult members of the Unification Church who sucked me in to their group with emotional love-bombing.[1] Soon I found myself in New York City. We had to sell flowers and candy on street corners, and were told to reach a quota, with fundraising the sole purpose of the cult hidden beneath a religious façade. And one night I stopped inside a bar to use the restroom when I caught the eye of a bad character. As he approached me, I ran out the door. And so did he.

Leaving my physical family to be in the cult was jumping out of the fire-pan into the fire. Though brought up in the Christian faith, the cult turned me to other gods and, with this, into the dark, occult realm of psychosis. Demonic voices surrounded me and attacked, accusing and denigrating. I had nowhere to go or anyone to whom I could turn. For three and a half years my life was a total nightmare until, finally, I was able to leave the cult and my parents got me help at a state-run psychiatric facility. The psychiatrist who reached out his hand to me that first day of meeting, unbeknownst, a devout Lutheran, became a lifeline for not only my physical and mental health, but for my soul as well.

1. Murphy, *Voices in the Rain*, 4.

Though in the depth of hell during the cult years I found that God had not abandoned me. One summer evening, as a thunder and lightning rain storm raged, and demons tormented me, a voice in the rainfall suddenly said: *Believe in Jesus Christ and you'll be saved.*[2] Turning to God in prayer, my answer came in the months to follow with release from the cult and being brought back into the nurturing community of the Midwestern town I had left only a few years before. Yes, I can say that I believe in second chances. Battling my shame and humiliation with the help of this kind doctor, I started to rebuild a shattered life. Having been destroyed mentally, physically, emotionally, and spiritually, God, in his mercy, brought something forth out of nothing. I will testify to the love and compassion of Jesus Christ, the author of my new life, new church family, and newly found faith.

❖ ❖ ❖

This book is to encourage a multifaceted approach to serious mental illness and health definitions as well as treatments through an integration of diverse perspectives which include the fields of Western psychiatry, psychology, and religion, and other cultural views from outside of the United States. All can make valid contributions given their various accomplishments and traditions. I believe there is much we can learn from one another. My intention is that my project will be a source of insight and healing for many and that it will equip the church, as well as secular psychiatry, to do a better job of enabling people living with mental illness to access the resources they need to recover, leading to a wholeness in personality and character.

To begin, no one has ever explained how the physical matter of a human brain can produce the nonmaterial aspect of the thoughts or abstract concepts which comprise the mind. Additionally, no one has explained how the *will* or decision-making can arise from material matter. This is a long-standing debate, nothing new. What is new is an exploration of the trinitarian construct of the physical brain, abstract mind, and shape of the soul. And that is what this book delineates, particularly with a focus on the importance of character or virtue, which according to historian of theology, Phil Cary, is *a habit or disposition or shape of the soul.*[3]

I point to how views of mental illness and health in both religious organizations and medical clinics can offer new holistic models and therapies for rehabilitation and renewal. During the past two centuries, doctors and civic leaders have limited their evaluation of the mental patient to either work-functional or disabled. It has been rather black and white.

2. Murphy, *Voices in the Rain,* 55.
3. Cary, See Appendix A.

Generally speaking, after some initial attempts in European countries during the 1700s–1800s for healing, restoration, and rehabilitation,[4] there has
been little progress. Specifically, in modern times in Iowa where I live, there
has been a lack of funding for such rehabilitation programs, and because of
this lack of resources mental health professionals have been severely limited
in what they can offer to those in their care.

Treatment providers would be wise to steer the patient toward holistic health. But what does it take to be become healthy holistically after
being destroyed by mental illness—mentally, emotionally, socially, and
spiritually? My intent for this book is to offer a resource for many within
the medical field of psychiatry, as well as those in religious communities on
a world-wide level, enabling a better job of supporting people who experience mental challenges during their daily lives. So, yes, what is referred to
as psychiatric illness in western society involves all of these: psychological/
social/biological/spiritual.

One preventable factor in serious mental illness is the problem of bullying; let's take a look at that. This is a common type of mistreatment which
is at the heart of many psychiatric diagnoses. Clinicians see many distraught
patients in the clinics every day due to this social problem. Not only does
bullying play a part in exacerbating emotional distress which often leads to
a mental illness; but on top of that, the stigmatization of the victim further
influences how they are treated by the general public which is most often
with discrimination.

Bullying comes in different forms: from cyberbullying, to pulpit bullying, to sibling bullying, to workplace bullying, the list goes on and on. Whatever form it takes, the consequences are deleterious for the victims. Victims
of bullying may lose self-esteem, productivity, general over-all health, and
experience mental health issues including depression often leading to death
by suicide. And for those who do not commit suicide some negative effects
can last an entire lifetime.

Bullying means that a [person] is intentionally causing another [person]
pain. That pain may be inflicted emotionally, verbally, physically, or electroni-
cally, and it is always harmful.[5] I grew up in a home environment that was
often combative. I truly believe my parents wanted to provide a good, safe
home, but despite their best efforts, it wasn't. From a very young age I faced
challenges having to do with personal space. When my siblings taunted
and tormented me, no one would intervene to stop the abuse. Therefore, I
became depressed. My schoolwork suffered as a result and I barely finished

4. Shorter, *History of Psychiatry,* 18–22.

5. Borba, *End Peer Cruelty,* 1.

high school. My bright smiles in youth photos betray the anguish I felt underneath and before the age of nineteen I ran away from home. It's true that many young people are off to college or involved in employment at eighteen; however, after giving tennis lessons for one summer and trying to attend college classes, I became incapable of functioning. My social skills were nil as were employment skills, and it was beyond my ability to apply for and land a job that provided a living wage. I could not support myself. So off I went when invited to and, subsequently swept up, into a cult.

Children need to know how to treat others in their family in a loving manner and not just externally in actions or deeds; but to simultaneously feel in their hearts that other people have value and worth. Since my life was devastated from the tumultuous events in my home in early years and my experience in the cult with the psychotic break, I was very unstable for most my adult life. One source of support I needed but lacked was a social network in the form of friendship which would include opportunities for me to learn the basics of civil interaction, but more than on a superficial level. I tried to find this periodically with attempts at socializing at Christian churches and Bible study groups but I just couldn't connect with anyone or make any friends. Though people were all around me, few wanted to get involved. My isolation felt almost as deep and hopeless as a convict in a solitary confinement cell. Unfortunately, I also made desperate attempts to find companionship with males, but these relationships were unhealthy and disastrous. Sexuality was not love. It was unfulfilling and emotionally destructive. I was estranged from my family because those relationships were dysfunctional and caused emotional distress. Without a strong support system, I could not learn the basics in how to interact and skills needed to become independent economically. But even though independence and autonomy are highly touted in our Western culture, one of the greatest lessons a person can learn in life is to accept that we are all interrelated and dependent on other human beings at times more so and, at others, less. As poet John Donne wrote in the seventeenth century: *No man is an island.*[6]

When I look back on the trajectory of my early life, what was the direction it took? And what kind of person did I become by my early thirties? Did I care? Did I have any insight? Did I have any interest in improving myself, my character, my constitution? I was not aware of having such an interest even though my success or failure as a human being probably depended on it. Unfortunately, there were traits and habits I acquired throughout my youth impeding my mental health. In addition, how did I view the surrounding world and my place in it? Danish philosopher, Soren Kierkegaard wrote:

6. Donne, *Devotions,* 394.

The more consciousness a person has of him or her being a self, the more will they have. And the more will a person has, the more consciousness of a self.[7] Applying this to my own life I can see that the more insight I gained and developed over the years, the more will I possessed to change, learn, and grow. *[A person] must become conscious of themselves as spirit or as such by the hard vicissitudes of life . . . helped to become conscious of themselves as spirit.*[8]

In my late twenties I was totally engrossed in a materialist survival mode: get a job and pay rent; get enough food. Try to find friends to decrease loneliness. Though I tried to attend worship services (impeded by a lack of transportation), a great amount of my mental focus was not on God or spiritual formation; instead, I focused on losing weight or trying to improve my appearance in other ways. I was a romantic and thought improving my appearance would help me find a permanent love relationship. I did not seek a male for financial support, but I was dead certain that *if* I landed a husband, I would never be lonely, and every other problem I had would instantly vanish—I would live happily ever after.

As the thirties rolled by, education came to the fore and I enrolled in more college classes (having made previous failed attempts directly after graduation from high school). But my emotional problems and episodic psychoses were insurmountable and I had to withdraw. My only success was in a writing class where I was commended by the instructor who urged me to seek a wider audience and to publish. But not succeeding in a more general education was very unfortunate because of the question: How can we think well or obtain mental integrity if we lack education? What place does education have in the scheme of things? I asked my friend, a college instructor, for his perspective on this very topic. See Appendix B for a brief summary.[9]

Then there was a string of paid employment opportunities and subsequent failures, including volunteer jobs leading to more failure. One health care professional I consulted thirty years later stated that, in his opinion, my early employment failures were mostly due to basic needs not being met, such as not having enough food, clothing, etc. I would add that I also didn't know how to conduct my life on a daily basis, including how to interact with other human beings in a civil manner or how to control my impulsivity. No one had taught me how. In my home where I grew up there was mostly conflict and derision. The entertainment industry certainly didn't help, nor did the types of people I associated with after I left the cult. What I know now but didn't know then, was that I needed to associate with good Christian

---

7. Kierkegaard, *Sickness unto Death,* 43–44.

8. Kierkegaard, *Sickness unto Death,* 40.

9. Scott R. Grau, "A Question of Education," Appendix B.

people, study the teachings of the Bible, and seek out a deeper personal relationship with Jesus Christ.

So fast forward to my late thirties when I finally gave up and made a nearly successful suicide attempt. Fortunately, at that time I lived near a church (within walking distance) and this put me on a spiritual journey of attending weekly worship services, Bible study groups, and frequent fellowship with Christian people. As it turned out, my heart, then, became set on knowing God, and I began to consider what kind of person I had become and what mistakes I'd made along the way. In addition, my growing faith led me to the question: What does God require of us? Did I have good character traits?

This, then, is the focus of this book. We take a good look at serious mental illness and human nature itself, the different aspects of being human, i.e., the emotional, intellectual, social, and spiritual components. We see how the dogma of science often tends to negate the supernatural aspects of the human being, and how secular psychiatry, therefore, negates a holistic recovery. When scientific materialism flattens or simplifies the reality of the mind, designating it solely to the realm of the physical brain, how is one to create a greater depth of heart and character, the mosaic of virtues and character traits? In short, to see what a well-rounded healthy human being looks like take first as an illustration its opposite, the *Diagnostic and Statistical Manual of Mental Disorders* (*DSM-5*) which is considered the experts' guide on mental disorders, pathology, or sickness, which has been used to improve diagnoses, treatment, and research.[10] The counterpoint to this is the development of mental health and *wholeness*—but from the unique perspective of someone who's been on both sides. For perhaps someone who's been first on the pathological side, (though it can be argued not always willingly so), can then honestly testify to the supreme value of a new multifaceted health.

I once had a friend who sent me an email saying that maybe my next book would be a recipe book (I had shared a recipe with her for my soup). I answered her: How spiritually perceptive you are! Yes, a recipe book is my new project—however, it is not about physical food. It has as its focus the different ingredients for good character and a healthy mind. Sort of the flip side of mental pathology. What is serious mental illness and what is a healthy mind, what is that comprised of? Mind, as in intellect, the state of the spirit/soul, personality, and character traits. And what does it take to reach that goal of good mental health, mental integrity? This, then, is the focus of my project: to take a good look at the root of problem and then to offer constructive solutions based on my experience, someone who is in recovery from serious mental illness and who's traveled along this road.

10 American Psychiatric Association, *Psychiatrists.* 1–4.

Chapter 1

Foundations

The Lord is my rock and my fortress and my deliverer,
my God, my rock, in whom I take refuge,
my shield, and the horn of my salvation, my stronghold.

Psalm 18:2 (ESV)

It is around 9PM on a cold, autumn Wednesday evening. I am sixty-six years old. As I was sleeping in bed in a totally dark bedroom, something startled me and woke me up. I abruptly turned my head on the pillow directly toward my closed bedroom door. There I saw what appeared to be a ghost, a spirit of male figure in a white doctor's lab coat, left arm lifted with his hand pointing—the trajectory of which went to a sign I had created many years before and taped to the wall: *Jesus is Lord.*

For some unknown reason I was terrified, and screaming, leapt toward my light switch on the wall, managing to flip the light on, but then I fell straight down to the floor on my face while my legs and feet remained tangled in the sheet and blankets. As I fell, my arm hit the small table next to my bed that held my Bible, cell phone, and clock—all of which crashed to the floor. I went face-down on the carpet. Then for the next few hours, I had vision problems. That morning my primary care physician's nurse wanted me to get checked out at the ER right away. There, a physician's assistant determined I suffered a concussion, facial contusion, and traumatic hematoma of forehead. He said the red scratch on my forehead was a carpet/rug burn; there was also a small area of blood on top of my nose. The physician's assistant told me to take pain reliever and said I should rest. Intermittent

1

pain continued for several months in parts of my head along with some mental confusion; exhaustion also.

The remarkable apparition of the spiritual being in a physician's coat had symbolic meaning. Christ, the great physician, is the great healer. God may not always use pleasant means to help us, but, also, painful operations or illness to change us spiritually. God can use any means he wishes to help transform a sinful person into a new creation. Often, the happy, joyful times do not change a human being. Some of the things we see as positive in life, do not always coincide with God's way of dealing with us for the improvement of our character. It can be that in the darkest valleys our greatest lessons are learned. So, this physician, in the night, came to direct me to the cross, his hand outstretched and pointing the way to the path I should take through faith.

It would appear that I should be wearing a crash helmet during my nights of not so restful slumber. I remember a sermon by a pastor many years ago; I cannot remember the exact date. Though the context is in a church sanctuary, I would add that encountering God unexpectantly can be experienced in any context, even someone's bedroom. The pastor quoted an extract from Annie Dillard's *Teaching a Stone to Talk: Expeditions and Encounters*:

> Why do people in church seem like cheerful, brainless tourists on a packaged tour of the Absolute? . . . Does anyone have the foggiest idea what sort of power we blithely invoke? Or, as I suspect, does no one believe a word of it? The churches are children playing on the floor with their chemistry sets, mixing up a batch of TNT to kill a Sunday morning. It is madness to wear ladies' straw hats and velvet hats to church; we should all be wearing crash helmets. Ushers should issue life preservers and signal flares; they should lash us to our pews. For the sleeping god may wake someday and take offense, or the waking god may draw us to where we can never return.[1]

So, take heed: *I will not leave you as orphans; I will come to you. Yet a little while and the world will see me no more, but you will see me. Because I live, you also will live. In that day you will know that I am in my Father, and you in me, and I in you. Whoever has my commandments and keeps them, he it is who loves me. And he who loves me will be loved by my Father, and I will love him and manifest myself to him.* John 14:18–21 (ESV)

So, again, why did this vision I experience involve a spiritual being wearing a physician's white lab coat? I believe it's because medicine is one

1. Dillard, *Teaching a Stone*, 40–41.

important dimension of human life. It can do things that the church cannot do and vice versa. We need both the church and the field of medicine; however, science can go too far, and that is when we need the theological view of morals and ethics to keep it in check. In regard to mental illness and health, a more well-rounded perspective of the brain and mind is needed that incorporates psychology and religious faith, along with Western psychiatry.

❖❖❖

Western psychiatry's view of neuroscience is built, fundamentally, upon dogma of science. A 2020 TV commercial stated the following: *The most certain thing in the world is science.* [Pfizer Inc., pharmaceutical corporation][2] For a person of faith, this is questionable because science has always had as its basis first of all, a foundation of basic assumptions. Many of these assumptions are no longer disputed in the general sense though there are always some lone wolves who differ in opinions. Science is considered by the majority as factual; these purported facts are based on theories. However, as many theories are considered factual based on empirical studies, some are, in reality, still unproven. Some things a scientist considers factual or what is purported as factual may, at times, consist of wishful thinking. In order to procure funding for research, scientists' claims of what is factual or what needs to be yet proven is strongly emphasized. For those outside the field of science theories may appear to be more of a science fiction or fantasy. It is beyond the scope of this project to delineate truth or falsehood in the great mass of scientific literature and, more specifically, about the brain. Instead, my focus in this project is on what can be known about mental health, development of character, and intellectual integrity from the standpoint of religion (which includes spirituality), and psychology without leaving out psychiatry. And subsequently, when it comes to mental health, what kinds of human beings can we become that supports our own wellness and prosperity during the course of our lifetime? My contention is that psychiatry's answer to mental illness is, by itself, insufficient when it comes to a view of what a holistic integrity of mind consists of and how it can be achieved.

In human beings, mental life is a decisive factor for abundant living. How do we maintain a healthy mental life? What causes the brain to break down or to become pathological, i.e., irrational, corrupt? Mental illness is a complex disorder with a multifactorial genesis. There is not just one cause; it has numerous contingencies. For example, it has been long held in contemporary medical practice that genetics and neurobiology play a part to make up what has been coined *a broken brain*. Psychology contributes by insisting

2. Pfizer Inc., TV Commercial, KCRG, 4/22/2020.

that individual thinking patterns—cognitive behaviors concerning rationality—have gone awry and can be fixed by therapeutic talk interventions. Both medicine and psychology have acknowledged the harmful effects of trauma and abuse sometimes experienced in the family while growing up, often resulting in years of emotional and/or mental instability and sometimes life-long disability.

From 1800 to 1900, in Europe, and then, the United States, there became a great influx of psychiatric patients flooding the medical system with the result of overflowing asylums. With a rise in alcohol-induced psychosis, there was a new proliferation of neurosyphilis that is believed to have produced psychiatric symptoms.[3] During the nineteenth century, it was posited that genetics and neurobiology play a major role in what constitutes a broken brain.[4] Germany, in particular, had places of learning that became research institutions serving the secular state advocating the authority of science.[5] However, mental illness is a complex disorder with a multifactorial genesis. There is not just one cause such as genetics in isolation. Unfortunately, many falsehoods have been propagated stemming from over-zealous research scientists in a hubristic race for recognition. As a correction, see the following which was stated by a University of Iowa psychiatry professor. This is what is currently known about genes in relation to mental illness up to the year 2020:

> What is definitely clear is that schizophrenia and other mental illnesses do not follow simple genetic models. That is that an identified abnormality in a given genes leads to disease. With schizophrenia it is thought that variations in many genes likely contribute to the risk of developing schizophrenia. The genetic changes can also interact with environmental factors that are associated with increased schizophrenia risk, such as exposure to infections before birth or severe stress during childhood.[6]

When pharmaceutical companies claim that nothing in the world is more certain than science,[7] how does the Christian counter such a notion? Afterall, our God, who seems distant at times and, who is quite invisible or nonmaterial, is what *we* claim as the foundation of *our* lives.

A diabetes medication put out by a certain manufacturer was recalled by the Food and Drug Administration [FDA] in 2020. This recall was due to

---

3. Shorter, *History of Psychiatry,* 53–54, 59.

4. Short, *History of Psychiatry,* 28.

5. Cary, *Meaning of Protestant Theology,* 220.

6. Del D. Miller MD, email to author, 7/19/20.

7. Pfizer Inc., KCRG, 4/22/20.

the medication's high level of NDMA, a carcinogenic.[8] Since this drug had been out for a number of years it could have damaged people's bodies. This was science gone wrong. The pharmaceutical industry was to blame for putting this product, created by scientists, on the market. Science is *not* certain. It can fail at times and do irreparable harm.

❖ ❖ ❖

If you wanted to find a book that is in direct counterpoint to my own work, Daniel Amen's *The End of Mental Illness* is a case in point. His subtitle says it all: *How Neuroscience Is Transforming Psychiatry and Helping Prevent or Reverse Mood and Anxiety Disorders, ADHD, Addictions, PTSD, Psychosis, Personality Disorders, and More.* Not only does Dr. Amen attribute mental illness and health solely to a physical material substance (the brain) with little spiritual attributes of the mind; he neglects the essence of being mentally healthy which is derived from the soul. He makes false claims such as there being no progress in psychiatry for the past seven decades (not true); and casting aside any humility, wants to remake something on a grand scale that he is only proposing from a limited, outside perspective (the objective observance of a professional), and, furthermore, from which he is drawing inaccurate conclusions. It is common knowledge that in any field, the ambitious often try to make a name for themselves and with this ambition will go to extremes. This is an extreme book. Even though Tyndale claims to publish from a "Christian perspective," Amen's book discredits that. Amen's book has little substantial biblical background and only touches briefly and superficially upon that which Christians hold in the highest regard: the life of the spirit, the soul. He neglects the spiritual world or realm (and beings), as well as a human's utter dependence on God's sovereignty, grace and protection, including Christ's role as healer, and Christ's witness of God's mercy through spoken testimony and acts as recorded in the Bible.

In contrast I am presenting an understanding of serious mental illness using a biblical foundation as background along with lessons learned from the wisdom (and failures) of Western psychiatry, things gleaned over the past 300 years, but with the added depth of insights from the field of psychology and the vital contributions of religion. This will provide a holistic frame of reference and support a broader healing paradigm than one solely focused on a simple neurology of the physical brain. In addition, social milieus within familial and civic environments influence the myriad of mental disorders and my thoughts address the micro aspect of one-on-one human interactions as well as macro connections within large communities.

8. Monaco, *Metformin Recall*, lines 10–11.

To decipher causes of mental breakdown and what promotes healing I acknowledge the importance of good nutrition for the human body and brain— and hopeful thinking—but take the reader further through the complex picture of what moral, ethical, and value-based character looks like when speaking about a stable mental integrity. Mental integrity, a healthy mind, is what I am concerned about, and this can only be formed by adopting the God-given resources undergirding the Christian faith built upon biblical truths. A prudent psychiatry will recognize this and partner with those who are seeking to help patients develop a godly character in tandem with logical and rational abilities. Right thinking, cognitive health, can dispel recurrent anxieties and other emotional problems because right thinking can promote a healthy lifestyle. Habits, patterns of healthy thinking based on good values, will create a healthy life trajectory, leaving an unhealthy one far behind; and it all starts with acknowledging God as the redeemer, protector, and sustainer of a healthy life.

So, wrong diagnosis, wrong cure. Neurology, *in isolation,* along with taking human beings out of social context, will not end mental illness because mental illness and health encompasses so much more than the mere neurological processes of the brain.

Russell Noyes Jr. MD, Emeritus Professor of Psychiatry, University of Iowa, is more lenient with the proliferation of scientific studies as he explains that the effort to explain the mind and its illnesses on how the brain works has been extremely limited and that in part it has been an effort to give psychiatry legitimacy as a medical specialty, the brain, an organ, where pathology is found. He says, not that efforts to link brain and psychological abnormalities are wrong; they have been useful. But as explanations for mental phenomena, they strip away what is uniquely human and what makes life meaningful. The focus on neuroscience has become popular and allowed many to say psychiatric disorders are real, thereby reducing stigma. But like emphases of the past (e.g., psychoanalysis, community psychiatry) Dr. Noyes believes Amen has gone too far.[9]

I was surprised that Dr. Noyes criticized community psychiatry. Perhaps he was referring to this branch of psychiatry used only in isolation. I had heard of this kind of work in my city to help the poorest of the poor. Community psychiatry sought to maintain psychological health in patients in more ways than just medication management, that is, in also including social supports. As described by Shtasel , Viron, and Freudenreich: Care providers in community psychiatry are "caring for an especially vulnerable subpopulation—homeless individuals with severe and persistent mental

9. Russell Noyes Jr, MD, email to author, 12/18/2020.

illness . . . this model teaches [health care providers] to think simultaneously at both the individual and the systems levels and enables them to understand the critical need to use nontraditional treatment approaches in order to provide comprehensive care for this marginalized population."[10]

I believe that since people with serious mental illness are not existing in a vacuum that to treat them as such is not only foolish, but nonscientific. Human beings exist in a multi-layered context that has great bearing on mental health outcomes. To just medically treat the brain to the exclusion of other areas of the person, is too narrow, and will not generate lasting outcomes. A doctor would need to be aware of the many factors involved that influence mental illness. We can find wisdom in community psychiatry as one of several programs and a holistic perspective it seeks to encompass will better enable doctors to treat the whole person.

Doctor Noyes further stated that he gathered that Dr. Amen is talking about things that can be done to a mentally ill person whereas I was talking about how the person should understand their illness and what he or she can do for themselves regardless of treatment. Mine is the perspective of the patient, Amen's more the therapist. Amen is saying the problem is all in the brain, so treat that. Doctor Noyes said that I am saying the problem involves other areas of one's life, i.e., beliefs, relationships, and values, which needs to be taken into account. Doctor Noyes felt Amen's approach was not wrong, but very limited, and may foster a passive attitude on the part of mentally ill person as they wait for the cure he is promising. [End of Dr. Noyes's comments.]

What I am saying is that if psychiatry is mainly concerned with only the physical aspect of the brain, then the whole field should be renovated. Therapists, psychiatrists, and psychologists, should give up this simplistic notion and if it means the death of psychiatry as a medical specialty, then so be it— though I doubt that is necessary. What we need, then, is a *collaboration* on the part of medicine to work with the other disciplines and fields to better treat the *whole* person, to treat the many facets of the human personality and/or mind, e.g., the social, emotional, spiritual—in collaboration. When I include *spiritual,* this is an invitation to the religious communities and hospital chaplains to have a place at the table.

I understand that currently medical psychiatry has to appease the powerful pharmaceutical industry which puts pressure on them to say it's *all in the brain,* and with this, the insurance industry starts making demands. So, perhaps the problem lies in economics and is not in the patients' best interests. What we need then is a transformation of the whole psychiatric

---

10. Shtasel, Viron, Freudenreich, "Community Psychiatry," Lines 8–12.

complex which would funnel more financial resources into whatever treatments have the most impact on the patients—and this includes psychological and spiritual interventions along with medicine—to better treat the whole person. But as long as we have state-run secular, scientific psychiatry then everything will be seen as only physical, and the insurance or administrative goals of economic constraints will put a strait jacket on those who care for the mentally ill.

So, no, my ideas are not just promoting *what patients can do for themselves*. Often, patients are too sick to do anything "for themselves." Often, patients need support from caregivers who have expertise in the various areas and disciplines I've mentioned. We need well-rounded professionals—professionals who are trained and educated to be aware of the multifaceted problems involved—who can then provide treatments for patients in a holistic manner and offer advice emerging from a collaboration of expertise in many fields.

What it all comes down to is this: When the mentally ill are initially incapacitated and thus unable to function well enough to get a job to support themselves; or unable to marry and be supported by a spouse; and, in addition, do not have family supports—who, then, will save them from homelessness? Throughout history, almost no one. When, in some cases, the family of origin is sick and is, itself, the source of abuse and disorder, then the mentally ill are without recourse. Without the family being healthy from which someone would normally obtain support, there is only homelessness, crime, incarceration or early death by exposure—the ultimate outcast given a death sentence.

And then medicine may step in with the mentally ill placed under the care and supervision of a physician. But I need to ask: Where is the church? The pastors, the congregants, etc.? I have seen modern-day ministers throw up their hands in frustration and say, "It's a medical problem! We'll outsource it!" It's true that Amen's book is giving psychiatry more of a medical persona but I seriously doubt that that was his motivation. It's true that with modern-day psychiatry at least there is a classification system for mental disorders which can help doctors judge which people should receive government aid in the form of disability benefits. The problem is, however, that the benefits are so scant a person cannot survive on them. So, you see people begging on street corners. Additional help has got to come from somewhere, and much of it comes from people guided by a spiritual orientation working at crisis centers or church-run food banks, along with the housing subsidy programs that provide limited support.

To avoid the serious and complex severe emotional disorders, beyond a physically healthy brain, people need the emotional support of godly parents and kind siblings during their formative years. The school system is also something to be considered, for even if the child comes from a good home, fraudulent, cruel teachers and bullying classmates can wreak havoc on a child's mental health. A good home and good school will feed the emotional side of the psyche and also stimulate intellectual growth and rationality. The church has a responsibility to teach parents in their membership how to be godly parents as well as how to teach their own children to behave. Then, with a healthy home environment mental illness is less likely to occur in its members. There are some cases for a child to exhibit mental illness even when the home appears to be near-perfect; however, this is rare and may be the result of outside factors such as classroom environments. For I maintain that along with the paradigm of the broken brain (which is also connected to the spiritual), there is the problem of behaviors—bad and harmful behaviors—that can only be lessened (though not entirely prevented) by parental education in a healthy home environment, one that has been fostered by Christian formation and education from within a strong religious community. Phil Cary remarked: Christian education is essential for Christendom's survival just as serious Jews know Jewish education is essential for their survival. But Christians don't always get that. We're too used to being carried along by Christendom, a nominally Christian culture that has an institutionalized respect for Christian faith.[11]

When considering the root problems regarding serious mental illness, there is the fundamental place of education which cannot be overemphasized—both, self-taught and formal schooling. I develop the concept of morals in connected with education, and their role in good mental health for individuals in chapter three. Touching upon it briefly here, I show its connection to classroom students in formal education, i.e., within our school system. Rodney Clarken states that:

> Moral intelligence refers to the ability to apply ethical principles to personal goals, values, and actions . . .The concept of intelligence generally refers to the ability to think and learn, and has been predominately used to describe the learning and application of skills and facts . . . most will agree that it is a general mental ability to reason, think, understand, and remember that draws upon the powers of learning, memory, perception, and deciding. Being moral is a complex, difficult, and lifelong process, as is developing moral intelligence. They both require conscious knowledge, guided by positive affect that is carried out in virtuous action. One cause of immorality is ignorance which

11. Phil Cary, email to author, 2/18/2021.

is sometimes manifested in blind acceptance of others' beliefs without adequately investigating the truth for ourselves.[12]

Blind acceptance of others' beliefs without adequately investigating the truth for ourselves? This is why it is important to have the skill of critical thinking when comparing different philosophies of life. When I blindly joined the cult, I did not have this critical thinking skill. This is where education plays a key role, both formal and individual. In my post-cult period, I only succeeded in finishing one year of college. Most of my subsequent learning which is on-going, was self-taught through reading and library studies.

Character strengths are important criteria for mental health and these fulfillments are not easily acquired but will often take a lifetime to achieve. Fulfillment of goals (some of which require character strengths or personality traits), must reflect effort, the willful choice and pursuit over time of morally praise-worthy activities.[13]

Making a deliberate choice to acquire good traits takes insight, time, and effort. For example, *self-control* is important. This type of thing allows people to override responses that hinder happiness or health and, further, to substitute or develop more adaptive responses. Self-control is a vital psychological strength that is crucial to personal well-being and, accordingly, should be amply cultivated and fostered.[14] For a significant part of my life I was impulsive and unreflective. In other words, I was intellectually and emotionally sick.

In part, my mental sickness persisted because I was largely cut off from the church. During my twenties and thirties, I did not have transportation to a Christian church. For a brief time, when I was married, I could have attended because we had a car, but my husband and I were involved in the non-Christian Unitarian Universalist Society in Iowa City. Fortunately, over my lifetime, I never turned to illicit drugs or alcohol in an attempt to escape misery. I know many of the serious mentally ill do this. I only smoked briefly when trying to fit in with other staff at a volunteer job for a couple of years, then quit; many people with mental illness smoke heavily during most of their adult years.

Without church attendance on Sundays, with the fellowship with other Christians—without this foundational connection to God—I floundered, and made unwise choices in relationships. I suffered humiliation and degradation as a result; and this further polluted my spirit. Gratefully, I had a Christian psychiatrist which helped me in some ways. But the most

---

12. Clarken, "Moral Intelligence," para 1.

13. Peterson and Seligman, *Character Strengths and Virtues*, 17.

14. Peterson and Seligman, *Character Strengths and Virtues*, 516.

significant problem back then was not having a deep and consistent involvement with other Christians and the church. I cannot stress deeply enough how damaging it is, mentally and spiritually, to be cut off from God in this manner. I hope my writing and shared experience can help others to know this truth that connection to the church is vital for mental health.

Another character strength I have found important is *persistence* which also has many benefits. It helps us reach difficult goals and along with that, an enjoyment of subsequent success. It can improve the person's skills and resourcefulness . . . it can enhance the person's sense of self-efficacy.[15] *Self-efficacy* involves the expectation of being able to exert control and perform effectively to bring about desired outcomes, and that sort of confidence may be especially enhanced by hard-won victories.[16] An example of reaching a hard-won victory was something I did in 2011 at the age of fifty-seven. After reading some literature on former reformers in the field of mental health, I decided to try some advocating in legislative action on my own. My state of Iowa was ranked then as one of the lowest states in the US as far of mental health services provided for the public. I thought I would push for legislative action for the increase of mental health services funding and establishment of new centers and facilities. To do this, I decided to put together some packets of materials and bring them to the Iowa State Capital for the legislators in the 84th Iowa General Assembly. I worked on the preparations for about seven months.

Initially, I contacted State Rep. Mary Mascher, who represents my area, and she guided me through the process. I needed and, then, successfully obtained, written support and permissions from some legislators, including State Sen. Pam Yochum—on up—through the capital leaders' hierarchy. I also sought and, obtained, clearance from the Capital security who were really very cordial. Getting all the required permissions from the capital leaders involved a lot of waiting and hoping. At one point—and it was on a hot summer day—I received the final permission. I felt sick (throwing up!), but relieved.

Meanwhile, at the University of Iowa Hospitals and Clinics, where I was working as a volunteer in the Patients' Library, I asked tenured faculty in the psychiatry department to sign a petition which included in a six-page document I had written stating that because of the dire conditions of the mental health conditions—specifically, lack of resources to treat the ill in the state of Iowa—we needed more funding for new programs and facilities. I was able to obtain some signatures of professors. In addition, I asked

15. Peterson and Seligman, *Character Strengths and Virtues*, 238.
16. Peterson and Seligman, *Character Strengths and Virtues*, 239.

an attorney if he would research and provide a legal document stating that what I was about to do was legal. I intended to include copies of my book, *Voices in the Rain*, as part of the packets. This was my memoir originally self-published in 2010, (Reprint, Wipf & Stock Publishers 2018). I included this legal document and, also, I found other information that also stated it was legal from another angle—I also included in the packet.

On the front of the packets, I put a typed label with each Senator's and Representative's name. My good friends from church, a senior couple, Dick and Penny Watson, agreed to take me to the state Capital (Des Moines) on the target date, January 9, 2012, (for which I acquired previous permission). It was the very first day of the 2012 Iowa General Assembly Session; the Governor did not appear and address the joint Session until January 10, 2012. It is interesting to note that Dick's father had been a Republican State Representative in the distant past. He and Penny had a child with mental illness, so they were eager for improvements in the state also.

Upon our arrival early that morning, we went through security with our boxes of packets on a dolly without a hitch. The House chamber official (Republican controlled) was very welcoming. However, upon reaching the Senate chamber (controlled by the Democrats), we encountered some resistance. I had to repeatedly show the official my permission papers until he relented. At any rate, I checked on things later on and found that all packets were distributed as requested on every legislator's desk in both the Senate and House. It's funny because maybe the chamber leaders had done research on my background beforehand and had seen my religious bent and as a result the Christian Right Republicans of the House supported my packets enthusiastically when I am actually a strong Democrat. And unfortunately, the Democratic Senate officials tried to stop my action when, in reality, I was on their side!

Out of courtesy, I also sent packet materials to the then top official, Governor Terry Branstad. Later on, I received a letter (and duplicate) from him with his thanks in which he shared he'd had problems with depression in the past.

As a side note: I had asked the St. Andrew Prayer Ministry for prayerful support for good weather since this was done in the first part of January and Midwest winters are known to be severe. As it turned out we had good road conditions for the two-hour ride to Des Moines and no precipitation. The temperature that day was in the lower-60s, an oddity for that time of winter. The following day, temperatures tanked and soon, in the days to follow, it snowed.

Not long after my advocacy at the Capital, Branstad closed down almost all of Iowa's mental institutions and cut other funding for the mentally ill. I asked Rep. Mascher if what I had done had not helped at all and said to me then that what I did was not, in reality, futile; but may still help in the long haul.

So, fast forward nine years. Progress has been made. Johnson County, Iowa, where I live, recently (2021) opened new centers/programs for helping the mentally ill. One is called the Guidelink Center which offers people with mental health crises and substance abuse problems diversion from jails and the ER. Also, about this time (2021), was the opening of the Crisis Stabilization Unit (CSU) at the University of Iowa Hospitals and Clinics. Additionally, it was announced (2021) that a faculty at UI in education would be receiving grant money to provide training in schools to recognize and help students with mental health issues.

I asked Dr. Michael Flaum (Emeritus Professor of Psychiatry, University of Iowa) about whether there had been any recent progress in recent years in the state of Iowa. Doctor Flaum, who has done a tremendous amount of work over the years to advance mental health care in the state of Iowa, answered the following: There is a lot going on and changing in the state for mental health and substance use—much more than I could cover here. Two highlights:

1. The Guidelink Center is just one of the *Access Centers* that are being developed. Recent Iowa legislation required the development of six access centers around the state.

2. Another is the addition of Certified Community Behavioral Health Centers (CCBHC's) which enhance the capacity of [psychiatric health professionals] to do crisis and other kinds of work. Several of these were funded in this last round.[17]

My former psychiatrist, Dr. Russel Noyes Jr. (Emeritus Professor, Psychiatry Department, University of Iowa Hospitals and Clinics), said to me that he thinks my advocacy was important; and so now I would like to emphasize why. It is because I have had serious mental illness, I have experienced its devastation, and I know how important treatment can be. I believe my perspective is unique, one that is rarely heard, and I hope people will listen.

I started to experience psychotic symptoms as a child. In addition, I felt rejected by all the relatives in my home which had a combative, emotionally (and, sometimes, physically) violent environment. My only refuge was public education and Sunday school at a Lutheran church. Other than these comforts, I basically grew up psychologically rejected and isolated. In

17. Dr. Michael Flaum, email to author, 7/15/2021.

my previously published books I describe how I got drawn into a quasi-religious cult, became severely psychotic, was hospitalized, and upon release, tried to make a new life for myself. Though I struggled with employment for many years, I was unable to support myself. My physical family only provided the bare bones, i.e., in helping me to obtain housing, and to get enrolled in government subsidy housing benefits, which did prevent homelessness. But I lacked the daily basic necessities like enough food or clothing which could have enabled me to pursue other goals. To keep my sanity, I avoided my family as much as possible. Unable to find emotionally warm female companions, loneliness was a major feature of my adult years which led to being emotionally and physically abused by unkind men, suicidal thoughts and gestures, and additional hospitalizations.

My psychiatric care began when I was in high school. I cut my wrists and overdosed on a bottle of Bayar. The doctor who treated me at the Community Mental Health Center then was emotionally cold and unsympathetic; but he did set me up with a psychiatric nurse counselor who met with me every few weeks. This nurse was kind and supportive and I think because of her care I was able to graduate from high school, though barely. After the cult and psychotic break, the medical support I received in Iowa City as an in-patient was crucial. There was still danger in being around my younger brother and he and my mother lived in an apartment where I had been forced to stay temporarily.

During my first hospitalization, the sympathetic psychiatric care providers helped me to get to the point where I was mentally stable enough to live in a newly established women's psychiatric half-way house. Without the care of these first doctors, nurses, and social workers, I would not have been able to do this. This was vital for my improvement and survival. Over the next many years, I had the support of a psychiatrist who saw me on a regular basis. I'm not sure if the old class of neuroleptics (anti-psychotic medications) helped my mental condition; however, with Risperdal/risperidone (starting in 1994), my condition did improve somewhat.

At one point, in my later years, I also saw a psychologist who supported me during a dark period, the years when the Governor had closed down many psychiatric facilities all around the state. I couldn't bear how the mentally ill were being treated by the government, or just in general, myself included. Finally, he was sent to China as the US Ambassador under former President Donald Trump. Then things began to slowly improve in Iowa for psychiatry.

I won't go into detail about all my challenges here. Please see my previous books. I just want you to know that, for me, psychiatric care was a life-line. I needed psychological support as well as medication. I needed advice on how to live and examples to follow. My transformation into a new healthier personality evolved over a period of many years; and without the help of doctors and nurses in the psychiatric field, I never would have made it. I am in their debt.

But so many people have not been able to access care. They have slipped through the cracks due to a lack of resources. Without any familial supports they end up homeless. They die of starvation—desperate, and alone. You can see them begging on the downtown street corners. The tragedy of millions of lives lost across the entire nation would have to be another project. I will only say here that preventative measures like the new crisis or diversion centers will help to keep people out of prisons. Stabilization centers will increase the chances of someone being able to gain a foothold. There is an urgent need to provide adequate housing for low-income people which will undergird their lives and give them a second chance. Or third. Or fourth.

Everyone deserves some help. God created all people to know him and to grow into a loving relationship with him. But without the basic necessities for day-to-day living, especially food and health care, people lose an opportunity for a better life. But, of course, that's obvious; and a society, if self-absorbed, will not meet the needs of the poor. Churches and other organizations must come to the fore. Psychiatry cannot do it alone. Let's all work together.

We must then consider financial foundations of those with serious mental illness. "Blessed are you who are poor, for yours is the kingdom of God . . ." Luke 6:20b (ESV) I have struggled with this Bible verse because as a low-income person living at the subsistence level, I have felt anything but blessed.

It is one thing to have physical health related to good medical treatments and supports derived from sound scientific research. It is another thing to have a strong religious faith to know what direction to take with our spiritual, mental, and vocational life once the body and mind are healthy. However, both medical support and your average church involvement presuppose that a person has the fundamental basics to begin with: food, clothing, and shelter. But suppose a person is born into poverty or later on in adult life encounters economic hardship that robs them of the necessities for daily existence? What then? What good is medical care if you don't have any food or you can only afford low-quality foods that will influence how you feel and function? How does the church support those in need?

There are certain basic financial foundations. Does the medical/scientific field and religious domain all interface with or influence the financial realm? When people are denied adequate income to undergird them, and then, in addition, medical care, I maintain this is an infringement upon their human rights; for without good physical health, a person cannot hold down a job to earn a decent living and contribute to society as a whole.

I was born into a lower-middle-class family. My parents eventually worked their way up by succeeding to obtain professional degrees and careers. My parents worked hard; they were not lazy human beings. They had four kids—four kids who didn't know how to get along—who fought and bickered almost daily. My mother was a woman of few words. And my dad was mostly absent.

When I needed help as a young adult my dad told me after his divorce and remarriage (he and my stepmom then had a combined total of seven grown children): "If we help one child, we have to help them all. So, we aren't going to help any." This meant that as a disabled adult I did not receive my dad's help. If I needed clothing—too bad, nothing was forthcoming, and I did not have the appropriate wardrobe for the workplace. If I ran out of food and needed help—no such luck. Transportation—forget it. My mom had her own financial problems and she struggled just to get by, herself. So, basically, I was out on my own. I did receive a meager amount of Supplemental Security Income (SSI), a governmental aid program which began in 1974,[18] but it was not enough to survive on. Fortunately, I had a strong work ethic, but lacking a college degree I could only obtain entry-level positions with minimal pay, and it was not enough. And, I learned that when I had new income from work, my benefits were subsequently lowered, so I never came out ahead; and therefore, I struggled to survive. It never occurred to go after men for their money and I never did. I had not read Jane Austin, so was not aware that women did that. I simply wanted a husband because I loved the man; not for any monetary worth. Most of my boyfriends were poor.

In my forties, in retrospect, I counted all my previous employment positions and came up with a total of twenty paid jobs. Twenty jobs I failed at except for a law research position which was temporary; in that, I succeeded. Add to this my numerous volunteer positions which were varied in duration. My therapist of later years told me that the way he saw it, I failed at my previous employment because I didn't have enough food to sustain me It was late in life I learned about Crisis Center food banks. I would add that I lacked social skills which could have helped me to make supportive friendships; so, I had little emotional support. My physical family added stress and serious mental health issues to my life, and they forced me to interact with them, but I did so with trepidation. Later in life I would gain some space and my mental health improved because of this.

18. SSA: Supplemental Security Income Program Description and Legislative History, para 2.

The environment we live in plays a part in our over-all mental health. It is helpful to have a neighborhood of healthy, productive, and positive people. Low-income areas have a mixture of people who strive to make a good life and the opposite, i.e., people who deal drugs, prostitution, and crime. I've mostly lived in low-income areas and have witnessed both kinds of neighbors around me. The following is an example of two kinds of people: someone who chooses to live in darkness and one who lives in light.

I have observed (observation is not the same as judging) two men about the same age who have the same types of jobs being operators of forklifts in different warehouses. One is a single man, and when not working at his shift it appears that he occupies himself by over-eating, drinking, and you can hear him doing laundry in the basement of the building; Generally, I would guess that he just sits around his apartment, very rarely going out except you will see him at the grocery store, or gas station. In addition, he is a heavy smoker and has, basically, taken a path of the iconoclast, rejecting all cultural norms and healthy ways to live, leading inevitably to self-destruction. As I mention in chapter three, *historically, self-slaughter or suicide has been judged lightly by many people who do not believe in God and also by pagan religions. It is even praised by such as these.*[19] *When a person wills for himself to be Lord over himself* [as in the concept of King Baby, you will see this term in substance abuse treatment circles], *this is defiance toward God,*[20] and is not accepting of *the idea of carrying a cross.*[21] His smoking permeates into the neighboring tenants' units, thereby poisoning the lungs of innocent bystanders until, finally, because of neighbor's complaints, the management forces him to go outside to smoke. Materialism, money, and food are the main focus of his life. He is obese and moves at the pace of a sluggard. *When someone is being too sensual/ sensuous he or she says good-bye to truth. If we say their self is a house, they are then just living in the cellar of the house in the determinants of sensuousness.*[22]

This man does not socialize, you never hear anyone visiting him and it appears he has no family connections. In addition, he is violent: slamming windows and doors, disturbing other people in the apartment building. And then he lurks outside at night, circling the apartment building, smoking and peering into windows as is made evident by the tell-tale tracks in the winter snow.

The second example is another operator of a forklift who has taken a healthier path. He is married with children, and has a cheerful disposition.

19. Kierkegaard, *Sickness unto Death,* 72.

20. Kierkegaard, *Sickness unto Death,* 111.

21. Kierkegaard, *Sickness unto Death,* 112.

22. Kierkegaard, *Sickness unto Death,* 67.

He is loving and kind as a robust member of a religious community. He writes complicated lyrical books on biblical characters which are then made public by a reputable publisher. He cares about his health and so he eats healthy food in moderation and maintains a healthy weight; is a non-smoker; does not abuse alcohol; and is physically active. He socializes with many friends and relatives and gladly accepts invitations for getting out of the house to visit with others on a regular basis.

Clearly these examples represent diverse pathways freely chosen by each man. One is healthy, the other is not. One lifestyle is well-rounded and shows mental integrity, having numerous interests outside the self and healthy thinking patterns. The other is self-absorbed and stunted, which leads, inevitably, to ruin and self-destruction. The man who is spiritually motivated has a transcendent quality and is most likely connected to God, the source of life and the giver of light. The other one, his opposite, is in darkness, or so it appears. These are human examples of light and darkness. So, what would be the relation between light and darkness? And what exactly is darkness and what is light?

Here is theologian Phil Cary's explanation of darkness:

Darkness gets used as an analogy to evil in the *classic* view of evil that I explain in my contribution to the book, *God and the Problem of Evil: Five Views*.[23] Like evil, darkness has no being of its own, but is only an absence of what is good. However, darkness in and of itself is not evil. It's only a bad thing when you ought to have light. So it's being deprived of the light you need that's the real evil. But still, the *real evil* in this case is an absence, a privation, not a thing in itself. For everything that has real being is God's creation, and God did not create anything evil. So, evil has to have the nature of absence, lack of what ought to be there, like darkness when you need light. This also means that black is not a good analogy for evil, because black is a real thing—a true color—as opposed to darkness, which is not a real thing in itself, but only an absence, a lacking of light.[24] Here is the relevant paragraph from my contribution to the book, *God and the Problem of Evil: Five Views*:

> It is easy to suppose . . . after all, that evil has a being of its own that opposes the good. This would make evil the contrary of the good, the way black is the contrary of white. But the classic view avoids this kind of black–and–white thinking. To put it in the sophisticated terms of medieval logic, evil is not the *contrary* of good but its *privation*. The term refers to a thing

---

23. Cary, "Classic View," 16–17.
24. Phil Cary, email to author, 2/13/2019.

being *deprived* of some good appropriate to the kind of being it is. If evil is a privation, then it is related to good the way darkness is to light, not black to white. Unlike black, which is a real color (for example, on a painter's palette), darkness is not something real in itself. It is only the absence of light or, we could say, light not being there. And to be deprived of light when it should be there, is bad. Hence one common label for the classic view, stemming from this medieval terminology, is the *privative* account of the nature of evil. It means not that evil is sheer negation (as if, absurdly, whatever does not exist were evil) but rather that evil is what takes place when things are deprived of some good they ought to have.[25] [End of Phil Cary's comments on darkness.]

Another example of the Kingdom of Light occurred one autumn day when I was immersed in the medical Christian community on a Sunday when I couldn't attend worship services at my church because it was closed to in-person attendance due to the COVID 19 pandemic. I had a new physical problem related to a salivary gland in my neck and was told to go to the ER. I was surrounded and immersed in the care and concern of some good people and I assumed some were Christians. Unable to be in my regular church community for a while because of the pandemic, I was spiritually starving. Then when at the hospital ER, the care and concern from the healthcare professionals made up for that. It was glowing with the love of Christ. I felt bathed and enveloped in the love of the Holy Spirit. Soon after, I learned that the day I was in the ER had been the feast of St. Luke, the physician disciple, Phil Cary informed me, and that his church got a nice sermon about how physicians and hospitals do what the church can't and vice versa.[26]

During the dark days and trials of the pandemic I thought: humans need to lift their hearts and voices to the heavens; set our minds and hearts on heavenly things, not the things of this world. Look to beauty, truth, love, joy, and peace. Look to God, upward from the cesspool of ruin and worldly corruption, focusing our every thought on what is good, true, and beautiful— healthy, right, and loving. Beauty. Colors. light.

I was emotionally withdrawn one Sunday morning at church before the pandemic and sat in meeting room with a window that allow viewing into the sanctuary. The worship service went on as usual. I had purposely left the lights dim in the meeting room. I felt rather cut off from the congregation emotionally then went into the sanctuary for communion and

25. Phil Cary, email to author, 2/13/2019; Meister and Dew Jr, editors. *Problem of Evil*, 16–17.

26. Phil Cary, email to author, 10/19/2020.

into Kingdom of Light. Dramatic change! Emotionally, energy, light levels. The church, the sanctuary full of God's people, is distinctly different—full of light, energy, a powerful energy force, the Holy Spirit.

I think the Rev. Dr. Timothy J. Keller is a wise Christian teacher. I had been listening to some of his audios/videos and I read one of his many books, *The Reason for God*. He is an American Presbyterian pastor emeritus, theologian, and Christian apologist who is the Chairman and co-Founder of *Redeemer City to City*, which trains pastors for ministry in global cities.

Here is something Tim Keller said about the seriousness of life which we would be wise to consider. He said (paraphrase): Victor Frankl, a Jewish doctor, wrote *Man's Search for Meaning* in which he was in a death camp during the second world war. He and his fellow prisoners had to decide if they would have hope or anything else meaningful to keep them going on a day-to-day basis. Some gave up all hope and quickly died. Some joined the other side and became evil. Some lived for a transcendent meaning and they survived.

Keller said that throughout our lifetimes we will all have *our little death camps,* i.e., grave illness, deaths of loved ones, loss of income or jobs, or other drastic problems that strip away what we formerly thought (erroneously) our lives were to be focused on. And it is then that we decide what we are ultimately living for and which direction we will go. This can happen many times over the course of our lifetimes. And that is why life is not just a little game to be played casually (as many young folks believe).[27]

I believe that for the ordinary life, marrying, having kids, career, living day to day a normal existence, all this can matter to the person and will be what motivates them, and they may not actively or consciously pursue what some call "meaning." However, whatever matters to a person or what they value in the long-term is the same thing as finding meaning. What matters, is equated with meaningful. So what matters to a person? And, therefore, what gives meaning to our lives? The ultimate thing would be if this meaning was in relation to God. A meaning with ultimate value could, potentially, sustain a human in situations of adversity, including, extreme adversity. In a desperate situation clinging to the thought of what is meaningful can be a matter of life and death, a matter of survival. I describe more of the theological and philosophical views on the importance of a meaningful life along with the implications in further chapters.

---

27. Keller, "Hope Beyond the Walls of the World," HKU.

Chapter 2

The Power of Influence

I deeply, passionately, loved my mother over the course of my life-time; but at the same time, I feared her. What I'm about to tell you is true. My mother gave me permission to write about our conflicts and before her death we reconciled, forgave, and assured our love for one another though it was an unusual kind of love. The beginning of our relationship was a struggle as the following will testify and which established lasting consequences.

OUR PERSONALITIES ARE IMPRINTED upon our souls before birth. How we were welcomed or not welcomed prenatally sets up our emotional patterns for life. Our mother's feelings for us during pregnancy influences how our mental or cognitive, and emotional development, turns out, in whatever direction, for good or for ill. For me, my default mode of feeling throughout my lifetime is that I am unloved or that no one cares about me. These emotions were set before the time of my birth. My father told me when I was an adult that my mother didn't want me. Third of four children, she doted on the first two of my siblings and then totally focused all her attention on my younger brother when he came along. I felt unwanted in my mother's womb. I heard that when she found out she was pregnant with me she made a special trip back to her physician and then went to see my grandmother, her mother. I was told her mother screamed at her in a rage, how could my mother do this? A third child was not welcome. My maternal grandparents only had one child. I felt this in utero, rejected and hated. All the emotions in my mother and those from other people directed toward her, affected me. I was despised. *Maternal antenatal anxiety and/or depression have been shown to predict increased risk for neurodevelopmental disorders in children, and to confer risk for future mental illness. Reports show that elevated levels of antenatal depression and anxiety [in pregnant women] are associated with poor emotional adjustment in young children.*[1] Anger is an emotion that affects the unborn as well.

All my life, my moods have been those of an outcast, the unwanted. My spirit and personality were shaped before birth. Even now, as an adult and Christian, the rejection is still etched in my heart. It is the default position of my moods and emotions. If the occasion arises when I might feel momentary happiness or joy, briefly, then the default state of being comes back and takes over. Some call it depression, even clinical depression.

The striking contrast between this hell and my first experience of church was what drew me to Christ my entire life. Saint Paul Lutheran Church in Davenport, Iowa, was, as I recall even as a toddler, a beautiful, majestic building with sunlight streaming through its windows and it was filled with the radiance of God's love. Sitting in the sanctuary for worship services with its grand hymns, and attending Sunday School as a youth, brought a feeling of security which became ingrained in my persona. It was my one escape from home. It was a new home, where the love of Christ was shared.

When I reached a certain age, attending school also brought comfort and a newly found security. The teachers were God's gift. They enveloped me with emotional warmth and acceptance; they valued who I was, just the way I was. As I grew up, my mother wouldn't talk to me (except on rare occasions). I don't think she realized that talking to children feeds them spiritually and intellectually, so I was starved at home. However, at school, the teachers talked to me, fed me, and I loved them for it.

Besides church, the school was a place of growth and development as a child of God. I was nurtured there. I found food for my soul and constructive tools to develop my brain. Later on, as adult I read parts of my mother's special journal created for her children's development. The part about me had only a few pages in the book filled out. She quoted my kindergarten teacher as saying: "Marcia is slow." My mother wrote that she responded to the teacher, "Marcia is lazy, and doesn't do enough chores around the house." I was five years old.

Though still immersed in a semi-depressive state, the gentle guidance from the school teachers opened new avenues for mental and emotional growth, and without this I would have been lost. What the school and its

1. Kinsella, et al., "Impact of Maternal Stress, Depression & Anxiety," 425–27, 437.

teachers valued then became my own values: orderliness or organization, reading, learning, writing, creating. To this very day in my senior years, I value these things the most in life, after loving God and my neighbor, the two greatest commands. Luke 10:27 (ESV)

Extending the discussion of the power of influence we go to how doctors, therapists, and counselors treat patients, the impact of these interactions on patients. Since therapists are only human and have their limits, it is unlikely that they will enjoy every patient they see. But at the same time, it is important that a therapist not overly criticize her patient because this has can have detrimental effects on the patient. Obviously, if the person who is taking care of a patient can see little positive aspects of the patient, this will impede recovery from illness. So, no matter how difficult it may be, it is important to try to find at least one or two positive qualities to build on. Everyone has gifts. What are the unique gifts each patient was born with? Counselors and therapists sometimes impede progress whether inadvertently or intentionally if they cannot find anything good to support.

Also, to prevent unintentional harm, health care and psychiatric care providers can take preventative measures by developing insight into their own behavior. Some ways of doing this are for the provider to monitor themselves by listening to their own voice, *its tone*, how they talk when addressing the patient, and I would add, to co-workers. Otherwise, left unchecked, the problem will go on indefinitely causing further harm to countless trusting and extremely vulnerable patients, many of whom depend on health care to survive. If the therapeutic relationship has problems over a period of many years, then the attempted cure (physical and psychological) can be worse than the illness and can, instead, exacerbate symptoms. This is also true in general medicine and the care providers there.

My first major psychiatrist for about twenty-five years sought to maintain the dignity of the therapeutic relationship. (See Appendix C for an essay written by Dr. Russell Noyes Jr. who elaborated on why he wanted to become a psychiatrist.) When he retired, the hospital truly lost a great soul. His kind are rare. After he left, it was challenging for me. This psychiatrist had expected a lot from me and encouraged my intellectual life, writing interests, and projects by giving a lot of support. Once, he even loaned me an important book that contributed much thought and information for my writing projects. His influence was great and really compelled me to seek answers to my life circumstances and mental health recovery. One strong point he made: "Marcia, when you are criticized, it makes you mentally sick."

I've never forgotten that. And criticism can be felt long before any words are directed audibly because we are spiritual beings. Being victims of bullying is a commonplace example. It affects us emotionally and spiritually and restricts our ability to function in a coherent way. As I mentioned earlier, I, for one, have been bullied and, as a result, I became depressed and confused and, on some occasions, psychotic. When asked to define the term *psychotic*, a leading expert in the field of psychiatry stated: "I would define psychosis as a loss of contact with reality, or difficulty telling what is real from what is not real. DSM-5 defines *psychotic features* as those characterized by delusions, hallucinations, and formal thought disorder."[2]

An example of how one person may influence another is highlighted in what is called the Pygmalion effect.[3] I would like to address the far-reaching implications that this effect has in psychiatry. How psychiatrists treat people with mental illness who seek their care has big consequences. Research on this effect appeared first in the field of psychology and then in the education field. Simply put, [the Pygmalion effect states that] when teachers expect students to do well and show intellectual growth, they do; when teachers do not have such expectations, performance and growth are not so encouraged and may in fact be discouraged in a variety of ways.[4] Physicists describe how what is being measured is changed by the presence of the person doing the experiment and by the process of measuring; that objects are influenced by the observers.[5] Physicist Eugene Wigner (1902–1995) held a subjective view of quantum mechanics stating consciousness of the observer, including the act of seeing, affects objects and experiments, influencing behaviors.[6] I believe that though quantum mechanics is on a micro-scale that the same can be true on the macro-level between emotionally sensitive and spiritual human beings. People influence each other emotionally and spiritually in their everyday lives and not just in an outward, visible way, but also mentally, either for good or for ill—even across great distances.

When a school teacher has little expectation for good behavior a student senses this, then the performance of the student suffers failure. The prophesy of the authority figure will be fulfilled for better or for worse. And I believe what happens in the classroom is replicable in the therapeutic relationship in psychiatric care, as well in other fields like sports, and familial interactions. Our expectations for people will influence how they perform, how they think and act. It is imperative, then, to think the best of individuals, to see them as possessing unique gifts and talents all their own and, along with that having potential for positive development, including the ability to change.

2. Del D. Miller, MD, email to author, 4/22/2016.
3. Rhem, "Pygmalion in Classroom," 1–2.
4. Rhem, "Pygmalion in Classroom," 1.
5. Carlson, *Quantum World*, Teaching Company.
6. The Information Philosopher, "Eugene Wigner," para 6.

As I mentioned earlier, a crucial shortcoming in temporary Western psychiatry is the notion of dividing the patients only into only two categories, either: disabled (not able to be gainfully employed) and non-disabled (can be financially independent through paid employment). What is missing is something in between: the notion of how we *facilitate healing and rehabilitation, a recovery process that progresses over time for those who cannot currently work but need help in being productive in alternative ways initially.* I say, *being productive,* because what is missing in mental disorder is a person's productiveness.

A major disruption in the therapeutic relationship is that sometimes, *there is actually no therapeutic relationship.* What constitutes healing? Do we need to turn from the masculine model of harsh discipline to a more traditionally feminine approach? Do the mentally ill all need surrogate mothers? I think not. But when a doctor fails to show compassion or encouragement and, instead, begrudges all the past wrongs and faults of a patient who has already previously endured overwhelming and unsurmountable traumas, then the progress in healing will never materialize. To put it quite simply: if a psychiatric practitioner lacks compassion, with whatever bias or prejudice, this will have a direct consequence of a very poor recovery response of the ill. In short: in order for a patient to respond favorably, they need compassionate care with *consistent* kindness. They've already been through the battlefield of familial and societal challenges while experiencing mental or emotional instability. What they need then is a taste of what it feels like to be loved and cared for, perhaps for the very first time in their entire lives. Often, for many patients without family support, the hospital or clinic is where they've first experienced someone's compassionate concern.

The relationship between a doctor or therapist and her patient is very similar to the dynamics between a teacher and student in a classroom. For example, in an educational setting:

> It would appear that we communicate something vital and undisguisable about our attitudes toward students and teaching in ways that transcend ordinary language. How we believe the world is and what we honestly think it can become have powerful effects on how things turn out. Study after study shows the Pygmalion effect even in laboratory animals. Researchers led to believe that one particular group of white rats is slower and less capable than another group of identical animals end up with results reflecting their beliefs to a degree that defies random chance.[7]

7. Rhem, "Pygmalion in the Classroom," 4.

Looking down on someone or using prolonged criticism is a form of bullying that has profound and long-lasting effects on the victims. Being bullied by my siblings and schoolmates while growing up, I then as a consequence, suffered from depression, anxiety, and withdrawal which led to loneliness. It changed my sleep and eating patterns and I lost interest in a lot of activities. In addition, I suffered from physical health complaints, decreased academic achievement—GPA and standardized test scores—and less school participation. As I withdrew socially, I missed, skipped, and nearly dropped out of school. I felt lower self-worth and these effects persisted well into adulthood.

Perpetrators are often those in positions of power (or who wish they were)—those who have a responsibility to promote the welfare of the those whom they see as inferior. When such abuses of power occur, all trust is eroded and victims are caught in a downward spiral. Much homelessness is a result of bullying when economic systems favoring the wealthy promote greed and cut-throat tactics throughout all areas of society, including the workplace.

Bullies can be those in any field who play hardball, who want to excel at all costs, to be number one and make a name for themselves, and anyone who gets in their way will be swept aside in an instant of narcissistic rage. Conversely, those who promote the general welfare of society may enter fields congruent with this goal, exhibiting a giving, positive nature, including empathy. How a person develops the virtue of compassion for the benefit of others is modeled in various places. It is obvious that if one doesn't learn this in the home environment in one's youth, it is imperative for religious organizations and schools to teach concern for the needs of others. The way people are treated themselves is one way they learn; and when children are bullied in the home this would obviously mean that other groups or organizations must step in to provide a model in what is missing. In some instances, mistreatment among growing siblings can cause life-long suffering. I know that my sibling's bullying harmed me deeply and caused life-long effects.

> Bullying means that a person is intentionally causing another person pain. That pain may be inflicted emotionally, verbally, physically, or electronically, and it is always harmful. Whether a person is bullying others, witnessing bullying, or the target of bullying, the behavior wreaks havoc on the victim's emotional, moral, and cognitive development; demolishes feelings of safety; and, if not stopped, can shatter lives. In fact, bullying is viewed as one of the most serious public health problems in the United States and Canadian school systems . . .

The effects of peer cruelty are far-reaching and can cause immense stress, anxiety, health problems, depression, and humiliation that may result in serious mental health issues for children. Bullying also induces fear and insecurity, which impacts students' concentration, academic achievement, and learning performance . . . In addition to homicidal violence, bullying victimization has also been shown to inspire youth suicide . . . .[8]

I grew up in a home environment that was mostly combative. I truly believe my parents wanted to provide a good, safe home; but despite their best efforts, it wasn't. From a very young age I faced challenges having to do with personal space. When my siblings taunted and tormented me, no one would intervene or defend me, and this went on for years at a time. Therefore, I became depressed. My schoolwork suffered as a result and I barely finished high school. My bright smiles in youth photos betray the anguish I felt underneath and before the age of nineteen I ran away from home. It's true that many young people are off to college or involved in employment at nineteen; however, after giving tennis lessons for one summer and trying to attend college classes I became incapable of functioning. My social skills were nil as were employment skills, and it was beyond my ability to apply for and land a job that provided a living wage. I could not support myself. So off I went, invited to and, subsequently swept up into a pseudo-religious cult.[9]

So, what has been the point of this chapter? It has described people and the ways we treat each other. It shows that this affects how we feel and what we become when treated in certain ways. Beginning before birth, how the fetus experienced welcome or rejection contributes to the development of its mental, cognitive, and emotional states; and as a child grows, what is the importance of authority figures society has put in place. Considering all these things, as I look at how the field of psychiatry over the past few centuries has searched for the etiology of emotional problems in the physical brain or body, and then has, subsequently, created somatic and/or social seclusion for the ill proved to be inadequate remedies. My focus in this chapter is not on the psychosis; psychotic episodes are another matter with a different etiology and presentation than depression, and I will address this issue in the latter chapters. There are many mental ailments and throughout history views on how to solve these issues greatly vary. *A Complete History of Psychiatry: From the Era of the Asylum to the Age of Prozac,* by Edward Shorter, details the various physical treatments in which the doctors tried to lift the spirits of the melancholic. Explicit in mirroring

8. Borba, *End Peer Cruelty*, 1,3.
9. Murphy, *Voices in the Rain.*

society's hard callousness of heart, a reviewer on the back-cover states that Shorter's book can be read for "entertainment" if one chooses. However, the suffering of millions is nothing to be laughed at. For more on the predicament of the mentally ill see my book, *To Loose the Bonds of Injustice: The Plight of the Mentally Ill and What the Church Can Do*.[10]

By far, the most comprehensive in-depth study on depression, i.e., despair, is Soren Aabye Kierkegaard's *The Sickness unto Death: A Christian Psychological Exposition for Upbuilding and Awakening* (penned in 1848; I prefer the translation by Walter Lowrie.) This Danish Christian philosopher and theologian wrote this masterpiece after having experienced first-hand his father's depressive states as well as his own.[11] Many in the European psychiatric field at the time postulated a genetic link between relatives of the those with depression.[12] Though it can be argued that the social behaviors within generations of families have continuous interaction patterns which develop illness in family members and which is thus compounded over successive years.

In the mid-1900s medications such as Valium, for anxiety, and Prozac, for depression, were over-prescribed as the answer to multitudes complaining of sadness, despair, and almost any other kind of daily problems with living.[13] But Shorter feels that, inadvertently, pharmaceuticals can be applauded for lessening the stigma of psychiatric illness when they espoused a neuro/biological cure for a brain disease in place of the wide-spread assumption of moral failure and bad character.[14]

A new medical development in the early 2000s, the Transcranial Magnetic Stimulation (TMS) is a noninvasive procedure that uses magnetic fields to stimulate nerve cells in the brain to improve symptoms of depression. TMS is typically used when other depression treatments haven't been effective. This treatment for depression involves delivering repetitive magnetic pulses, so it's called repetitive TMS or rTMS.[15] During an rTMS session, an electromagnetic coil is placed against your scalp near your forehead. The electromagnet painlessly delivers a magnetic pulse that stimulates nerve cells in the region of your brain involved in mood control and depression. It's thought to activate regions of the brain that have decreased activity in depression. [Psychiatric professionals claim] that though the biology of

10. Murphy, *Loose the Bonds*.

11. McDonald, *Kierkegaard's Life*, 74.

12. Shorter, *Complete History of Psychiatry*, 28–29.

13. Shorter, *Complete History of Psychiatry*, 320–23.

14. Shorter, *Complete History of Psychiatry*, 324.

15. Mayo Clinic, *Transcranial Magnetic Simulation*, lines 1–5.

why rTMS works isn't completely understood, the stimulation appears to impact how the brain is working which [providers claim] decreases depression symptoms and improve mood.[16]

I maintain that it is not the electrical stimulation at all that occasionally "lifts" a depressed patient's mood. I believe that many depressed patients are extremely isolated and starving for attention and that being given this personal attention in a clinic with hands on treatments are a counterfeit dose of healing, a placebo. Just getting out of the house, having somewhere to go (they were invited to), where they are *welcomed*, and being around other human beings is in itself therapeutic. And then after the appointment, the patient might stroll down to the hospital's Café to get a snack or meal which also lifts the mood. This medical treatment does not really get to the *source* of despair, which has a non-material, non-bodily or psychological cause.

For an in-depth look at sources of destress that influences our attitudes toward daily situations we need to consider one's particular outlook on life and how we see our place in it. For the way we view the reality of life itself, our perspective, will directly influence our fluctuating moods, whether we experience despair, and over-all mental stability. Kierkegaard's *Sickness unto Death*, is a treatise on despair stating that *without understanding spirit it is impossible to understand despair,*[17] because *despair is . . . a sickness of the spirit,*[18]*and the spirit is related to the eternal.*[19] Kierkegaard continues: *This points to the fact . . . that man, regarded as spirit, is always in a critical condition—and if one is to talk of despair, one must conceive of man as spirit.*[20] *This [despair] is the most dangerous sickness of all if one does not wish to be healed of it.*[21] When a human is not conscious of themselves as spirit, often the *hard vicissitudes of life* helps him or her to become conscious of this.[22] A person, when they reach the end of their rope and are in the darkest depth of despair, they may come to believe there is a God and that they, themselves, *exist before this God.*[23]

Our daily activities and habits deeply influence how our emotions are experienced. For example: what we read has a big effect on the psychological state of the mind and emotions. If we read mostly horror novels and

16. Mayo Clinic, *Transcranial Magnetic Stimulation,* lines 1–18.
17. Kierkegaard, *Sickness unto Death,* 34.
18. Kierkegaard, *Sickness unto Death,* 35.
19. Kierkegaard, *Sickness unto Death,* 36.
20. Kierkegaard, *Sickness unto Death,* 37.
21. Kierkegaard, *Sickness unto Death,* 39.
22. Kierkegaard, *Sickness unto Death,* 40.
23. Kierkegaard, *Sickness unto Death,* 40.

gruesome literature that is about death, murder, and violence, and which is full of profanity and immoral scenes, we would be foolish to think it has no effect on us. Many people who read this type of literature eventually succumb to suicide, unfortunately, even at a young age. Conversely, literature that enlightens and promotes healing can be very helpful for those who suffer from depression. Seeking the good in the world and literature can lift the spirits.

Chapter 3

Morals and Character Development

They are the code we live by in a civil and just society. They are what we use to guide our interactions with others, with our friends and family, in our businesses and professional behavior. Our values and morals are a reflection of our spirituality; our character. They are what we hope to model for our children and the children around us, because children do watch us as they develop their own sense of right and wrong. Everyone knows their importance, don't they?[1]

THE FIELD OF PSYCHOLOGY suggests that when individual thinking behaviors—cognitive behaviors—have gone awry that they can sometimes be fixed by therapeutic talk interventions. At the same time, both medicine and psychology have acknowledged the harmful effects of trauma and abuse which subsequently result in years of emotional and/or mental instability and sometimes life-long disability.

The religious sector maintains that human beings consist of body, mind, and spirit, and each influence the other for good or for ill in over-all health. In the field of philosophy certain epistemological schools of thought maintain that morals and ethics play a part in intellectual virtue and will play a part in forming and maintaining good, sound mental health.[2] *Our intellectual life is important for the simple reason that our character, the kind*

---

1. Donelson, "Values and Morals," lines 1–8.
2. Wood, *Epistemology*, 21.

of person we are and are becoming is at stake. Careful oversight of our intellectual lives is imperative if we are to think well, and thinking well is an indispensable ingredient in living well.[3] I believe that failing to oversee our intellectual life can lead to disaster. And I believe that the further a person strays from virtue, intellectually and morally—including emotionally and behaviorally—this would lead to a corruption of one's thinking processes, thus leading to a disorder of the mind, e.g., some forms of mental illness, and consequently, sickness of the soul.

I believe that the further one strays from morality and virtue, mental health deteriorates in the degree or proportion of the separation. Christianity is a saving faith in more ways than one. For as it has been demonstrated throughout the centuries: *It's either Christ or madness.* An example of a person rejecting Christ in favor of atheism and immorality is the late nineteenth century German philosopher and cultural critic, Friedrich Wilhelm Nietzsche (1844–1900) who for approximately the last ten years of his life was insane.[4]

Therefore, in some instances (not all), it can be argued that a breakdown in mental health is often preceded by a breakdown in morals. One cannot be separated one from another; in what order this occurs is debatable. There are other situations in which external environmental factors often play a part in causing mental illness and are outside of one's control.[5] I touched upon this in chapter two.

One example of mental illness resulting from a personal emotional chaos is in Anton T. Boisen's *The Exploration of the Inner World*, (originally published in 1936), where Boisen chronicled his own crisis involving human relational conflicts combined with problems in his religious outlook. He only regained some periodic mental stability after resolving such conflicts, simultaneously being bolstered by his faith and it took many years of struggle. Boisen experienced a religious awakening in the course of his schizophrenic illness. This story took place in the context of the late 1800s to early 1900s, a time in American history when there were few effective treatments for psychiatric illness. Boisen, by the strength of his will, struggled to overcome his mental illness using his reasoning combined with religious faith.[6] Anton Boisen is the pioneer founder of the clinical pastoral education movement.[7]

---

3. Wood, *Epistemology,* 17.

4. New World Encyclopedia, "Nietzsche: Breakdown," Lines 1–20.

5. Lurhmann and Marrow, *Our Most Troubling Madness,* 201–3.

6. Boisen, *Exploration of the Inner World.*

7 .Leas, *Biography of Anton Theophilus Boisen,* line 1.

My understanding of Boisen is that an unsuccessful romance was a primary contributor or even instigator to his mental health crisis. Boisen and I had different kinds of schizophrenia. According to accounts, he did not have hallucinations like I did but, instead, suffered from catatonia which is described in a psychiatric manual as: behavior [showing] a marked decrease in reactivity to the environment. This ranges from resistance to instructions (*negativism*); to maintaining a rigid, inappropriate or bizarre posture; to a complete lack of verbal and motor responses (*mutism* and *stupor*). It can also include purposeless and excessive motor activity without obvious cause (*catatonic excitement*). Other features are repeated stereotyped movements, staring, grimacing, mutism, and the echoing of speech.[8]

The term, *schizophrenia* or *schizophrenia spectrum,* is such an ambiguous term—there are so many kinds with so many different symptoms listed in The Diagnostic and Statistical Manual of Mental Disorders, Fifth Edition (DSM–5)[9]—that I believe it renders the term invalid. As mentioned in Chapter 2, I am more inclined to say I suffered from an experience of psychosis in the sense that I heard voices or what science calls hallucinations, i.e., visual and auditory phenomena.

I came to a conclusion independently when I wrote an article (1997) describing what Walter Houston Clark also mentions in his *The Psychology of Religion*[10]—that we know the validity of a religious idea or claim of reality, including an event as to whether or not it originates in God, by the *fruit*, as I put it.[11] The Bible states we know a tree by its fruit: a good tree cannot produce bad fruit; nor a bad tree, good fruit, Luke 6: 43–45 (ESV). Clark uses the increase in *personal efficiency*[12] as a test as to whether personalities with historical importance had as their inspiration a godly source.

So, then, we ask the question: is what people are personally believing theologically or philosophically making them more efficient, more competent, and fruitful? Are they getting things of good quality accomplished, i.e., thinking more clearly, and being more productive? I know in my case that, among other things, my personal religious faith helps me to persevere. And with this perseverance, I am able to reach some goals, and experience some limited success. When I become frustrated due to blockages, either from physical illness/pain, or emotional, economic, or social problems, my faith reminds me that God doesn't promise an easy life. Quite the contrary,

---

8. American Psychological Association, *DSM–5*, 88.

9. American Psychological Association, *DSM–5*, 87.

10. Clark, *Psychology of Religion*, 361–62.

11. Murphy, *Collected Writings*, 38–43.

12 Clark, *Psychology of Religion*, 361–62.

to take up our cross and follow Christ requires self-denial, sacrifice, and to experience hardships.

Some have expressed that people can be restored to good health. I agree with Boisen's idea that sometimes the psychosis is constructive in the sense that an improved condition can be reached.[13] That we would see in some transformative cases a new creation, something better than before. This is a theme that runs through basically all Boisen's writings. And this is certainly how it was in my case because I was psychologically ill since childhood and needed to be made new. The psychosis and crisis as a young adult gave me a new life, but it wasn't instantaneously done, like magic. Recovery has been a years-long process and continues as a process that is developing over time. One difference between myself and Boisen is that I had very little health to begin with that could be restored whereas, he appears healthy initially.

A connection to the church will help a person reprioritize their values and goals. My lifestyle over the years went through a transformation. Unfortunately, for many years, I worshipped idols in various forms. An idol is anything that takes the place of God in our lives, be it a place, person, career, or thing. According to emeritus pastor and author Timothy J. Keller:

> A counterfeit god [idol] is anything so central and essential to your life that, should you lose it, your life would feel hardly worth living. An idol has such a controlling position in your heart that you spend most of your passion and energy, your emotional and financial resources, on it without a second thought. It can be family and children, or career and making money, or achievement and critical acclaim, or saving "face" and social standing. It can be a romantic relationship, peer approval, competence and skill, secure and comfortable circumstances, your beauty and your brains, a great political or social cause, your morality and virtue, or even success in the Christian ministry . . .There are many ways to describe that kind of relationship to something, but perhaps the best one is *worship*.[14]

As a young and vulnerable teen, I ran away from a home that was full of emotional and physical violence, and away from the Christian church I was confirmed in. I joined a quasi-religious cult which was idol worship. But an idol cannot help us. When the leader of the cult claimed he was a perfect human being and was the Messiah, and demanded that followers bow down and worship him, I went along with that to try to fit in because I was lonely. And I became psychotic. See my memoir, *Voices in the Rain:*

13. Walters, "Religion and Psychopathology," 126.
14. Keller, *Counterfeit Gods*, xviii.

Meaning in Psychosis for this first-person account. Later on, after I escaped from the cult, my focus in life continued to be somewhat warped. In addition, poverty and lack of social support compounded my struggles. I tried to attend worship services at various denominations, but lacked transportation. Since intellectual (or mental) integrity is closely tied to moral character, in retrospect I believe I needed the church which can potentially provide Christian formation and education.

In a general sense, right now in the twenty-first century, more than ever before in history, because of increased wealth, leisure, and mobility among the middle (and even lower) classes, it appears that there is a culture of rampant sexual immorality, hedonism, alcoholism, and pleasure-seeking, as well as on a global scale. These lifestyles can cause a lack of intellectual integrity leading to increased mental instability or mental illness of all kinds. And to compound the problem there is a decrease in the number of psychiatric care facilities, clinics, and providers, so fewer receive treatment which leads to more mentally ill who are incarcerated for often minor offenses and who then end up homeless and on the streets.

I believe that morals and virtues have their genesis in God's purposes for humans. Phil Cary teaches that God's laws and commands are for the good purpose of bringing us to God in the kingdom of God.[15] He says this is called the *teleological* view of human nature and without this view, God's commands don't make sense.[16] Cary goes on to explain the summum bonum, which precisely is the goal of the commandments:

> Summum bonum is Latin for *highest good*, and strictly speaking, that designates God. But it can also refer to the highest good *for us*, and then it designates our union with God together with our neighbors: what the Bible's New Testament calls the Kingdom of God and eternal life. *Good*, in Thomas's Aristotelian philosophy, always has the aspect of a goal, something to be desired. Therefore, in Thomas' philosophy the Law cannot be the supreme Good because every valid law serves a purpose or goal higher than itself. You don't obey commandments for their own sake, just because rules are rules. Every good rule or law is valid insofar as it rightly serves a higher purpose. So the law of the land, if it is any good, serves the common good. Likewise, the law of the Kingdom of God serves God's purpose of bringing us together in eternal life and happiness with him—the common good of the Kingdom of God—which is in fact the ultimate good for human beings, the summum bonum. The twofold Law of Love

15. Phil Cary, email to author, 3/06/2020

16. Phil Cary, email to author, 3/06/2020

thus commands us to be the kind of people who aim for and enjoy that union: the kind of people who desire union with God as our ultimate good and desire that our neighbors share it with us, and who put that desire into practice. The practice and work of that second desire, wanting our neighbors to have the same supreme good that we desire, is what it means to love them as ourselves. That's basically Thomas Aquinas' view, which is not much different from Augustine's. I think it makes a pretty good summary of Christian ethics.[17]

So, do we value a relationship with God and our neighbor? And how do our life choices reveal what we value? William Zeller, a psychiatrist states:

Values are everybody's business; yet they are very personal. They emerge at all levels of life and enter into all that we think, feel, and do. In a sense, personal values are ideals or standards that give meaning to our existence. They serve as guides for our behavior and give direction to our strivings. Thus, they are of great concern to those interested in human motivation and behavior. Usually associated with moral and spiritual matters, values are considered to be in the province of the philosopher or the clergyman, but since they are closely associated also with psychological matters, they are of major importance to psychiatrists whose task it is to understand man and the way he functions in sickness and health.[18]

(and help patient decipher their own values quote here)

If we value loving God then we try to obey God. Emotions come and go. They are fleeting. How we conduct our lives says more. God gives his commands in the Bible, his word. In Exodus 20:1–17 we find the Ten Commandments. And the New Testament lessons teach us how to obey. Through the parables and words of Christ and his followers clear directions are given. They center around loving God and our neighbor. Who is our neighbor? All the people around us; no more, no less.[19]

The importance of education, study, libraries is this: When the pandemic forced the closure of our local and University libraries, I died. This was another form of death. It meant so much to me. Books, librarians, study, teachers: Without this, I cannot live day to day. Learning and growing is fundamental to my existence. I often pray for a teachable heart.

17. Phil Cary, email to author, 2/26/2021.

18. Zeller, *Religion and Medicine*, 256.

19. Murphy, "*More God*," 17.

I asked Prof Cary: Study is a luxury and so many people are just trying to find food and shelter (on a global scale). So, I see character formation and moral teaching to be a sort of luxury for those who have ample time to devote to it. But I suppose even the starving will encounter times of moral decision-making. What is your slant on that?

Phil Cary: It seems to me that everybody undergoes moral formation. Sometimes it's moral deformation, like when children are raised in abusive homes. But that does form their character, alas. The flip side is that a good home forms character in good ways, and this does not require formal education. And included in this moral formation is instilling a love for wisdom (the true meaning of *philosophy*) which includes a desire to know the truth and developing habits of good judgment—all without formal education. In every town and village in the world, school or no school, you can distinguish between people who want to understand the world around them and fools that don't care to understand. That's just human nature. People naturally love to study, because by nature they love learning for its own sake. Studying can't come first on the list of necessary activities, however, because first you need food and shelter and clothing. But once they get to the point where they have a little free time and energy left over from necessary work, people start wanting to learn, just for the sake of learning—and also, as blacks in the South obviously realized, for the sake of exercising political power and responsible citizenship. Higher education is just an extension of that deep-seated need. It's called *liberal* education because it's education for free people, not slaves (liberal—same root notion as liberated). But a liberal education is not widely possible for people who don't have enough to eat—or who are so worried by economic [in]security that they can't take time to learn for the sake of learning. When that happens, you get job training but not study—as often happens today. Still, the natural human desire is for study, for learning the truth about the world for its own sake. For we are creatures made in the image of God, which means all of us by nature desire to know.[20]

I answered: You have a much more optimistic view of human nature than I do. But that would be great if all people had the desire to know.

Phil Cary replies: Yes, I'm resolute about that. Anyone who does not desire to know has been warped in some way: abused, bored to death at bad schools, or maybe is a morally vicious fool. But to prefer ignorance to knowledge is not in our nature, except insofar as our nature is corrupted by sin and suffering.[21] [End of Phil Cary's comments on learning.]

20. Phil Cary, email to author, 11/18/2020.
21. Phil Cary, email to author, 11/18/2020.

Fulfilling our God-given purpose and choosing a meaningful direction in life are derived from our choices in what we value mentally, emotionally, spiritually—day to day and moment by moment—which in turn, guides our activities. So how then can we define values? Again, from Zeller:

> Very simply, a value is our own personal estimate of what is desirable; it is our judgment of the worth of an endeavor. Many factors determine and influence this idea of what is desirable, so that we make our judgments of worth on various levels in the order of relative importance. We are free to choose from among alternatives those things that hold the greatest value for us. We thus establish a hierarchy or scale of values with respect to personal, intellectual, artistic, political, economic, social, and ethical matters . . . On our personal scale of values there is always the choice of what is good or what is not good for us.[22]

One ethical aspect on the spectrum of virtues for mental health is courage, taking a moral stand for some belief. Alexandr Solzhenitsyn, Russian author and dissident, delivering a commencement address for Harvard University on June 8, 1978, remarked that he saw a lack of courage in the West and asked the question: *Why do we lack courage?*[23] And as Peter Kreeft puts it: why are we afraid of suffering?[24]

How is being courageous a form of integrity? Courage consists of being intellectually honest, devoid of self-interest and hidden agendas. It is when you go against the grain, being armed with integrity. It means standing up for the truth when persecution is certain. Courage is defending Jesus Christ when it is not popular or politically correct. It is conscientious deliberation of the various options to see what faults and discrepancies come up. Courage is giving deliberate deep and comprehensive thought for the discovery of falsehoods and deceptions. It is when we support truth when it is not comfortable or convenient and when a backlash is certain.

Courage is what Christians in other countries have when they know that attending a church service will mean their private home could be destroyed by arson or they, themselves, and their wife and children could be murdered. Courage is Rev. Dr. Martin Luther King Jr., sitting in a jail cell because he stood up for justice. Courage is the opposite of private hoarding of security and no risk taking. It is facing the music of hateful opponents at the risk of your career and life. Courage is the opposite of playing it safe.

22. Zeller, *Religion and Medicine*, 259.

23. Solzhenitsyn, "A World Split Apart," para 12.

24. Kreeft, *Ethics: History of Moral Thought*, audio CD.

Standing up for truth in a fallen world calls for intellectual and moral honesty that faces dangers and calls for emotional sacrifice.

Denying Christ as Lord is not courageous but is the embodiment of cowardliness. Lest you think I boast, I, too, once thought "all religions are equal." My ignorance needed to be corrected and my willful naivete eliminated. Studiousness, an intellectual virtue,[25] proved to be one of the avenues that revealed the light. People who remain in darkness have often willfully chosen the darkness out of self-interest or in blatant rebellion against God. Christ clearly calls us to deny ourselves, to take up our cross. Courage consists of these things, not in denying the truth or turning our back on the Holy Trinity, who alone reigns.

Concerning ethics and what is good, take these true-life illustrations of people I know of.

One young man is born into a wealthy family in an urban big-city in Iowa in the early 1990s. He has a father who is a nominal Roman Catholic. The young man has everything given to him and more than he could want. As a result of his being pampered, he can't do well in college or the workplace because he doesn't have a work ethic and doesn't respect authority. He is morally bankrupt, a conniver, sexually promiscuous, becomes an alcoholic, and uses illicit drugs, then is dealing for quick thrills. His father pays for him to go into an expensive drug rehab in a posh California suburb. His life is ruined and he feels no remorse or purpose for his life and is suicidal. His wealthy father constantly bails him out and prevents prison time with expensive lawyers.

Take the opposite, also the story of a man who had a Roman Catholic father: In the 1940s, in rural Iowa, he, as young child, has to use an outhouse in the backyard for a bathroom. The house his grandparents lived in had a cellar with dirt floors. And his older relatives had to cook with a wood-burning stove. He works from a young age and pays his own way through a Catholic high school. When his classmates prod him to be on the basketball team (he is very tall), he counters with, "I want to go to college, so I am working to pay for it." He does go on to college and graduates. He is morally conscientious and has a strong work ethic, maintaining steady employment. He respects authority, i.e., medical, civic, and the hierarchy in his church. He fights for the rights of the underdog, and says he is willing to serve jail time for his convictions.

Those who do not believe in a God and that they can have a personal relationship with this God are rejecting the very life source upon which they depend. They are severing the limb upon which they unconsciously cling.

25. Wood, *Epistemology*, 34.

And eventually, when a crisis comes and distress is paramount, the choice to live or die will face them in the form of a temptation to commit suicide.

Kierkegaard believed that the act of suicide is a moral choice, contrary to what we see declared in modern psychiatry (that of physiological origin). And Kierkegaard said that killing oneself was ultimately *defiance toward God*[26] and *the goodness of existence.*[27] It is a *crime against God.*[28] When the medical answer is to use a nasal spray in the emergency room, to medicate despair, what is this saying to the suicidal patient? That the despair of the spirit, emotions, and heart are just chemical properties in the brain? (see chapter 2 end) Instead, Kierkegaard wrote that one needs to change from being *a fatalist who is unable to pray and is without hope*[29] to, in all humility, humbling oneself under *the hand of the Helper;*[30] being open to change in the situation that comes from the all-powerful God[31] with whom all things are possible. Matt 19:26 (ESV). *Possibility is for the self what oxygen is for breathing.*[32]

And research to find a genetic link in suicidal people: What does this imply about humans? That we are just deterministic mechanical machines with no spirits or free will and are under the control of physiological genes? When the notion that possibilities are lacking for our lives, this can, and often does, lead to despair.[33] *Determinism and fatalism are spiritual despair in which there is no imagination. With these the person lacks the possibility of faith in order by God's help to be able to deliver oneself from certain destruction.*[34] Despair and the act of suicide is the ultimate defiance. A person chooses not to humble herself under the problem in faith.[35] Historically, *self-slaughter or suicide has been judged lightly by many people who do not believe in God and also by pagan religions. It is even praised by such as these.*[36] *When a person wills for himself to be Lord over himself* [as in the concept of King Baby—will see this term in substance abuse treatment circles], *this is defiance toward God.*[37]

---

26. Kierkegaard, *Sickness unto Death*, 113.

27. Kierkegaard, *Sickness unto Death*, 118.

28. Kierkegaard, *Sickness unto Death*, 73.

29. Kierkegaard, *Sickness unto Death*, 62.

30. Kierkegaard, *Sickness unto Death*, 114.

31. Kierkegaard, *Sickness unto Death*, 114.

32. Kierkegaard, *Sickness unto Death*, 62.

33. Kierkegaard, *Sickness unto Death*, 57–58.

34. Kierkegaard, *Sickness unto Death*, 63–64.

35. Kierkegaard, *Sickness unto Death*, 114.

36. Kierkegaard, *Sickness unto Death*, 72.

37. Kierkegaard, *Sickness unto Death*, 111.

And speaking of *King Baby*, there is a biblical story in the Old Testament about a historically verifiable king named Nebuchadnezzar who was very prosperous. The biblical texts say he took full credit for the success around him and his arrogance was punished by insanity brought on by God. Those who self-worship, and put themselves in the place of God, will be humbled. What happened when King Nebuchadnezzar took full credit for his kingdom's prosperity is as follows: At the end of twelve months he was walking on the roof of the royal palace of Babylon, and the king answered and said, "Is not this great Babylon, which I have built by my mighty power as a royal residence and for the glory of my majesty?" While the words were still in the king's mouth, there fell a voice from heaven, "O King Nebuchadnezzar, to you it is spoken: The kingdom has departed from you, and you shall be driven from among men, and your dwelling shall be with the beasts of the field. And you shall be made to eat grass like an ox, and seven periods of time shall pass over you, until you know that the Most High rules the kingdom of men and gives it to whom he will." Immediately the word was fulfilled against Nebuchadnezzar. He was driven from among men and ate grass like an ox, and his body was wet with the dew of heaven till his hair grew as long as eagles' feathers, and his nails were like birds' claws. Daniel 4: 29–33 (ESV).

Fortunately, there is a happy ending because after a time period, when Nebuchadnezzar lifted his eyes to heaven, his reason returned to him. Daniel 4:34, 36 (ESV). His position and the glory of his kingdom was restored to him and he said: Now I, Nebuchadnezzar, praise and extol and honor the King of heaven, for all his works are right and his ways are just; and those who walk in pride he is able to humble. Daniel 4: 37 (ESV).

I asked Phil Cary about this debate: Some people think that humans can't learn to change bad behavior to become better humans. But then we would not have Christian formation in churches or schools. There would be no point in disciplining your children. Right?

Phil Cary said: We change all the time. It's just that changing for the better is much harder than changing for the worse. The disagreement, I suppose, is about *how* hard it is, and how far we can change. It's a lot like recovering from physical wounds. We don't always fully recover.[38]

I believe that in order to change for the better we need to acknowledge the spirit within us and to hope for what is eternal, taking comfort in this as that which can supersede much of the turmoil and crisis we encounter in our everyday lives.

---

38. Phil Cary, email to author, 5/27/2021.

Chapter 4

Mental Illness in World Cultures

"The battle against the Devil is the principal task of
St. Michael the Archangel. And [it] is still being fought today."

—St. John Paul II, May 24, 1987

WESTERN PSYCHIATRY DOES NOT acknowledge the spiritual realm in regard to psychotic phenomena. With the exception of the psychiatrist, Dr. M. Scott Peck's work, a trailblazer in bridging psychiatry with spirituality, hallucinations are discounted as meaningful in any real phenomenological sense. What I mean by that is simply this: psychiatry, as a science, only sees hallucinations or psychotic phenomenon as neurological manifestations of bad wiring within a broken brain. This is understandable when we see psychiatry embedded in the scientific field of medicine, a physical or hard science.

However, no amount of reasoning can take the place of real-life experience.[1]

As a person who has experienced psychotic phenomena, I will give testimony to the very real spiritual manifestations of a nonmaterial realm; a realm where I was attacked in a significant way and this attack was impactful, having an immediate effect upon not only my mind and emotions, but the rest of my entire life. There are some other cultures around the world which do not have such a negation of spirit as does Western science and psychiatry. Other cultures, in places less advanced perhaps in technology

1. Kelsey, *Other Side of Silence*, 41.

or other modern sophistication, have a fundamental respect for the unseen world where forces impinge upon human beings in their everyday lives. I set about gathering information on some people there who experience mental illness, people who are fighting to survive amongst the various mental influences, who sometimes find religion and religious community helpful, counterpoints to those in Western society where medications are solely administered and psychotherapy treatments predominate. My intellectual explorations in this area are part of my personal experience in living and have worth, I maintain, as legitimate thought and are part of who I am as an author which I wish to convey in writing and have value as such.

In the following text I offer a glimpse of the plight of the mentally ill from a non-Western perspective. Does this have implications for us in the United States and Europe? Yes, and profound ones at that, not only for those who have afflictions of psychiatric disorder, but for the societies that are struggling to help these people in their day to day lives. The religious communities of the Jewish and Christian faith traditions are to be at the vanguard in helping the mentally ill whether as doctors/therapists and nurses or pastors and lay people. And as more knowledge about the various sources of mental disorders is disseminated better supports will arise to help those so afflicted. Other cultures with their different perspectives have unique proposals for cures and supports which we, in Western psychiatry, can learn from. I know I would benefit from some of these supports, myself, and will describe them further along in this chapter. I will explain how in my own healing story (which is on-going), I would like to see the church open its doors to new ways of supporting the mentally ill in a pastoral setting, ways that have succeeded in other places around the globe, contributing to my own holistic recovery as well.

So, yes, academia, as well as the general adult population, can learn from diverse cultures and various worldviews. Take, for example, the field of chemistry: *Integrating indigenous and Western views can provide students with insight into using multiple perspectives. Cross-disciplinary knowledge offers ways to solve problems more holistically and to promote respect for different worldviews.*[2] Even though this excerpt has the perspective from chemistry [concepts from general and organic chemistry], I believe this integration of worldviews applies to multiple fields of academic and medical contexts.

With the aim of learning about situations in a limited number of different cultures I sent some emails to international medical and general mission personnel asking for information regarding their experience with exposures to individuals with mental illness in the cultures where they were situated.

2. Zidny and Eilks, *Integrating Perspectives*, 1.

The time span for the content of their information covers the mid–1900s to the present day (2020s). The following pages provide a view from these professionals regarding some of the situations for those who either were or were not given a formal diagnosis in the city or region where they carried out their work. I explained to them that my intention is that my project will be a source of insight and healing for many and that it will equip the church, as well as secular psychiatry in civic institutions, to do a better job of enabling people living with mental illness to access the resources that they need.

In the process of gathering information from a limited number of sources on an international level from former and current missionaries along with professors, church representatives, and medical mission personnel (physicians), culturally indigenous interpretations of psychiatric phenomena are considered, as well as how various cultures deal with mental illness within familial and societal contexts. I asked for, and received permission to identify some of the responders and others are stated as *anonymous*.

My first set of quotes are from a response given by Douglas J. Tilton who has been based in South Africa (Durban, Cape Town, Johannesburg) for over twenty-six years. At the time of this writing, he has also had responsibilities for accompanying partners in Lesotho, Zimbabwe, Mozambique and Madagascar. Over that time, he has worked with peace structures in KwaZulu-Natal and spent a decade with the South African Council of Churches (in their Parliamentary Office and also the General Secretary's office). At the time of this writing his current position was Regional Liaison for Southern Africa. In that role, he related to the Presbyterian Church (USA)'s global partners in five countries, supervised PC(USA) mission personnel in the region, and did resourcing for congregational and presbytery partnerships. He has also had a role in resourcing PC(USA) advocacy initiatives relative to the whole continent of Africa.

Marcia Murphy: What are your impressions regarding native people who have had a mental illness, what were the symptoms or behaviors they displayed? What was the ill person's beliefs and interpretations regarding the symptoms?

Douglas Tilton: I have not really had much experience with mental health issues or personal contact with individuals living with mental illness in South Africa in the course of my work. But I have at least one person that I know that I believe to be living with mental illness, though it has never been properly diagnosed as far as I know. This friend is not a *native* South African, but an asylum seeker from another African country. He manifests what I, as a layperson, presume to be symptoms of some form of paranoia and/or schizophrenia (e.g., he hears voices, believes that other people—including strangers—are conspiring against him, etc.). This has led him to make what I would consider to be bad life choices, making it difficult for him to hold employment, causing him to say inappropriate things, often alienating those who want to help him to do better. Occasionally, he will acknowledge the voices as a problem or admit that he is not convinced that he can trust the things that they say or encourage him to do. But mostly he does not. Though he has suffered a lot as a result and now effectively lives on the street, he remains surprisingly optimistic about life for the most part, though he launches angry email volleys from time to time, blaming various people and institutions for his plight. On some occasions when he has seemed to experience his illness as a problem, I have tried to identify community mental health resources that might assist him, generally without much success. There certainly are mental health services in the Western Cape, but these can be difficult for someone living on the streets to access, particularly without much support.

Marcia Murphy: Were there any family members who shared their perspective on what they believed mental illness was? How did this affect their loved one, e.g., detrimental or helpful (as far as you could tell)?

Douglas Tilton: My friend does not have any immediate family in South Africa. He did have a cousin working in Johannesburg at one stage who tried twice to find employment for him.

Marcia Murphy: What do people do to combat mental illness? What efforts are made to treat the mentally ill person? Do they have clinics and/or physicians to go to? If so, what do the doctors prescribe as far as medications or natural substances or activities/procedures?

Douglas Tilton: South Africa certainly does have fairly good awareness of mental health issues and (I believe) pretty good facilities for diagnosis and treatment for those able to access them. However, those with more limited means get shunted into failing, overtaxed and under-resourced care systems that (I surmise, though I have no direct knowledge) are especially poor at dealing with rarer or less visible or well understood ailments, including mental health concerns. There are many factors that shape mental processes and behavior, ranging from brain chemistry to genetics to environmental factors to nurture, etc. In the USA and many western industrialized societies, dominant cultures don't often include things like witchcraft or spirit possession in the list of factors considered. In South Africa and many African societies, these are often seen as sources of socially aberrant behavior. But I suppose that they are no more *external* than, say, an abusive father would be as a source of disruption to mental health . . . or even a substance abuse issue.

Marcia Murphy: Are the mentally ill treated as outcasts or integrated within families and the communities? What activities (if any) do the mentally ill participate in during a normal day?

Douglas Tilton: Okay, let me leave South Africa now, because I think that on this question, I can say something more interesting and potentially more useful to you about Madagascar. I do not have direct personal experience with people living with mental illness in Madagascar, but I want to share a bit about the ministry of the PC(USA)'s partner there, the Church of Jesus Christ in Madagascar (known by its Malagasy acronym, FJKM). The FJKM is a large church of about five million members, and it takes a very holistic approach to ministry.

One very interesting aspect of the life of the church in Madagascar is that it has a branch of service, alongside elders and deacons, known as the shepherds (*mpiandry* in Malagasy). The shepherds are part of the church's "revival movement" (*fifohazana*)—a feature that the FJKM shares with other Christian churches on the island. The shepherds have a ministry of spiritual healing. (Some visiting Presbyterians from the USA have dubbed them, "Stephen Ministers on steroids"!) One of their major functions is to run spiritual retreat centers, known as *tobys* (pron. TOO-bees), around the island. A bit like some Presbytery church camps in the US, the shepherds from different congregations will take responsibility for running a particular toby for a few weeks each year. The idea is that people come there for prayer and healing. The thing that fascinates me is that the tobys are seen *both* as places where people who are experiencing mental illness *and* those who simply want to go on retreat can go, at the same time. Thus, the church actively brings together populations that, in the USA, we often try to keep very separate. Part of the reason for this is that many of the behaviors and syndromes that we in the USA might attribute to mental illness, folks in Madagascar are more likely to see as the result of malevolent spiritual forces. In some places, they talk specifically about *spirit-related disorders* either as distinct from or as a complicating factor in mental illness. People experiencing these issues go to the tobys with members of their families who stay with them, prepare meals for them in communal kitchens, and support them throughout the process. The shepherds hold worship and healing prayer services several times a day, provide pastoral care and counseling, and maintain the buildings and grounds. People can stay as long as they feel that they need to . . . for free! Illnesses for which people seek treatment vary widely, including such disparate problems as alcoholism and autism. [End of Douglas Tilton's comments]

I will now make some comments pertaining to a previous statement by Douglas Tilton, that many of the behaviors and syndromes that we in the USA might attribute to mental illness folks in Madagascar are more likely to see as the result of *malevolent spiritual forces*. In some places, they talk specifically about spirit-related disorders either as distinct from or as a complicating factor in mental illness. I will now share some thoughts here regarding malevolent spiritual forces.

Western theological or philosophical scholars usually avoid debates as to whether there are such beings as evil spirits. However, Saint Augustine claimed—that in the beginning of the creation of the world, fallen angelic beings rebelled against God's authority and central place, thus elevating themselves as the center—but this is considered by scholars, an *intellectual exercise,* in other words: speculation or conjecture. But for those who hold the Bible as a legitament source of historical truth, there is solid scriptural support of the existence of real spiritual angelic beings that were and have been actively in rebellion against God and who, in addition, conspire to cause problems for human beings. For one who respects biblical authority, see, for example: Jude 1:6 (ESV) *And the angels who did not stay within their own position of authority, but left their proper dwelling, he has kept in eternal chains under gloomy darkness until the judgment of the great day.* Also, Rev. 12: 7–10 (ESV) of a battle between good angels and bad the time of judgement: *Now war arose in heaven, Michael and his angels fighting against the dragon. And the dragon and his angels fought back, but he was defeated, and there was no longer any place for them in heaven. And the great dragon was thrown down, that ancient serpent, who is called the devil and Satan, the deceiver of the whole world—he was thrown down to the earth, and his angels were thrown down with him. And I heard a loud voice in heaven, saying, "Now the salvation and the power and the kingdom of our God and the authority of his Christ have come, for the accuser of our brothers has been thrown down, who accuses them day and night before our God.* And, Ephesians 6:12 (ESV) *For we do not wrestle against flesh and blood, but against the rulers, against the authorities, against the cosmic powers over this present darkness, against the spiritual forces of evil in the heavenly places.*

Morton Kelsey, who was an Episcopal priest, counselor, and contemporary author of books connecting religion and psychology states the following: *Probably the foremost reason most people today cannot believe in angels or demons is that Western man has let his ability to know, his idea of science, mislead him into doubting the existence of any reality which he cannot touch or understand. Non-material reality, then, cannot exist. The creed which underlies this point of view can be stated rather plainly: There is only matter and the laws that govern it. The psyche is merely an epiphenomenon of matter.*[3]

---

3. Kelsey, *Reality of Spirit World*, 2.

Kelsey continues with how *Christians in ancient times believed in the nonmaterial, spiritual realm; and to the writers of the Bible's New Testament, including a major figure, the Apostle Paul, as well as Jesus Christ, the world of these spiritual entities was very real indeed. Men were beset by beings from the spiritual realm which has elements of both good and evil in it. If man is to escape being overcome by evil elements, the forces abroad in the world which seek his destruction, he must take real religion seriously . . . .*[4]

One of the valuable contributions from Douglas Tilton's observations is the part about the spiritual retreat centers called the tobys in Madagascar where both mentally ill persons and non-ill people gather for numerous days of prayers of healing and worship. I believe that the spiritual discipline of daily prayers and Sunday worship are a vital part of my own healing. We've also had healing services at my church which take about an hour, but not very many in recent years.

I know somewhat what it's like for people around the globe who do not have medications available to them. Because often during hot Iowa summer days, when the extreme outdoor temperature reaches over one hundred degrees and I have been unable to keep my medications from being destroyed inside my apartment which is also unbearably hot, I have gone without this medical help but only temporarily. Being without medication for a day or two, and experiencing psychotic symptoms I may know what it is like for others around the globe who, daily, year-round, do not have any psychiatric medications at all. I believe there are some protections from malevolent spiritual forces often gained from the neuroleptic drug coating of the neurons in the brain, cushioning the mind from the outside forces and without this, God's help is crucial. But with or without medication, God's help is crucial, but for a person without any medication at all for an extended time, it is even more critical.

❖ ❖ ❖

The following questionnaire response is from someone I met through the church I've been involved in: Prof. Bernard Adeney-Risakotta, Professor of Religion, Ethics and Social Science, International Representative ICRS, Indonesian Consortium for Religious Studies, UGM, UIN SUKA, UKDW, Yogyakarta, Indonesia.

Bernie Adeney-Risakotta: Unfortunately, I have little experience with mentally ill persons in Indonesia. I can give a brief general answer rather than specific answers to your questions. There is very little professional mental health care in Indonesia. People with mental illness are usually cared

4. Kelsey, *Religion of Spirit World*, 20.

for by their families. Yes, there is a stigma and they may be kept secret. A rather striking manifestation of mental illness among people who cannot be controlled by their families, is nudity. In Indonesia, women especially dress very modestly, but mentally ill men and women often go without clothes. It seems to be a sign of the ultimate casting off of social taboos. Mentally ill people without much or any clothing are usually ignored by the general public. Since the weather is warm, nudity doesn't endanger their health. One other comment is that most people believe in spirit possession. Some mental illness may be interpreted as spiritual possession. This may not be considered negatively as evil spirits, but positively as a special gift to act as a medium for the ancestors or other benevolent spirits. Of course, a spirit may not be benevolent but rather neutral or evil. Some of the above matters are discussed in my new book: *Living in a Sacred Cosmos: Indonesia and the Future of Islam* (Yale Southeast Asia Studies, 2018)[5]

Marcia Murphy: Maybe the mentally ill there who do not wear clothes cannot afford clothing, have no resources because they are in poverty, so they are unable to obtain adequate clothing.[6]

Bernie Adeney-Risakotta: Marcia, you may be right, but I doubt it. Indonesians are very modest and families will do anything to get their mentally ill members to wear modest clothes. But they take them off. I see it as a rebellion against the rules of society. People give them clothes, but they take them off and abandon them. I had a cousin (from my wife's Javanese family) who was a young Muslim woman and wore very conservative Islamic dress. She had a bout of mental illness and refused to wear any clothes at all. The family did all they could to keep her dressed and at home. Fortunately, she recovered and was able to return to her studies. The main *safety net* for mentally ill persons in Indonesia is the family.

One terrible practice is frequently carried out by families who cannot keep their mentally person at home or guard them against nudity, self-inflicted wounds or hurting others. They chain them up inside the house so they can't go out. My university, including colleagues from the Department of Psychology, have induced the government to conduct a nation- wide campaign to forbid and do away with the practice of chaining up mentally ill people. Two of my friends and colleagues are professors of medical anthropology at Harvard university. Profs. Bryan and Mary Jo Good, work with the Psychology Department of my university here, doing research on mental illness and its treatment in Indonesia. They have been part of this campaign against chaining.

5. Bernard Adeney-Risakotta, email to author, 7/23/2018.
6. Marcia Murphy, email to Bernard Adeney-Risakotta, 7/27/2018.

If someone is naked, it is a clear sign of mental illness. People ignore them, not to be cruel, but so that they will not be shamed. In a shame culture like Java, being naked is a great shame. By ignoring a naked person, they think they are being kind. But at the same time, they deny the person, perhaps the one thing they want most: to be noticed. All of this is complicated by the common belief that we are surrounded by spirits who may possess some people. Most people believe that spirit possession is real. It is not necessarily considered evil. Someone who is possessed may have a special gift for communicating with the ancestors. In that case, we should listen to what they say, even if they are naked![7]

[End of section with Bernie Adeney-Risakotta's comments]

As someone who has observed the mentally ill and who has had direct experience with them, I have come to the conclusion that an evil spirit possessing a human being is a real phenomenon. Spirit possession is real. Western psychiatry and culture, with the exception of particular religious groups, deny this fact. I, for one, have seen it. It has existed in very close proximity to me in people at the places where I've lived and worked at.

For example, from my observations of neighbors who live nearby, i.e., in my apartment building or relatives in my family, I'd say that the marks of a possessed person are a loss of consciousness, not being faint, but not having any insight into one's behavior, mostly behavior which is usually malevolent and harms himself and/or others. The possessed do not have a conscience when they inflict harm; and have no empathy when they cause other people to suffer. They, instead, take delight in the suffering of others. For a possessed person is not conscious of one's own self or in one's boundaries with the world. It is denial of the self as a personality that would normally have self-discipline and control over one's actions. This is a state of having no self-discipline, self-direction or purpose. Possessed people will focus on cigarettes, and smoke them almost without ceasing (or whenever possible) during all waking hours. And they might abuse alcohol and other illicit substances because this self-destruction is acceptable to them, life has little worth. As such, they have rejected God and live in the ultimate defiance of God and God's commands. They are governed by philistinism. Philistinism *is being guided by materialism and is disdainful of intellectual or artistic values.*[8]

If they can hold down a job, their lifestyles are totally centered around the job, performed as routine in repetition, without imagination. Self-isolating behavior is the hallmark of possession as are anti-social behaviors. Destructive violence, both physical and emotional, in the home is

---

7. Bernard Adeney-Risakotta, email to author, 7/27/2018.
8. Wikipedia, "Philistinism," lines 1–3.

normative for them, striking out against relatives/partners and breaking furniture and/or injuring other persons in the home. Their personalities are belligerent and hostile and will strike out at anyone, e.g., neighbors, or anyone around them.

The possessed reject usual norms of modesty in dress as well as other moral behaviors. Possession also destroys original thought, imagination or creativity of the intellect. The human is under control of the alien force and performs the directions mandated by the demon or demons. Multiple possessions by many demons are possible in one human and is described in the Bible's New Testament:

> Then they sailed to the country of the Gerasenes, which is opposite Galilee. When Jesus had stepped out on land, there met him a man from the city who had demons. For a long time he had worn no clothes, and he had not lived in a house but among the tombs. When he saw Jesus, he cried out and fell down before him and said with a loud voice, "What have you to do with me, Jesus, Son of the Most High God? I beg you, do not torment me." For he had commanded the unclean spirit to come out of the man. (For many a time it had seized him. He was kept under guard and bound with chains and shackles, but he would break the bonds and be driven by the demon into the desert.) Jesus then asked him, "What is your name?" And he said, "Legion," for many demons had entered him. And they begged him not to command them to depart into the abyss. Now a large herd of pigs was feeding there on the hillside, and they begged him to let them enter these. So he gave them permission. Then the demons came out of the man and entered the pigs, and the herd rushed down the steep bank into the lake and drowned. Luke 8: 26–33 (ESV).

The goal of the dark forces that possess humans are to destroy the one possessed and to also harm others: to persecute and harass non-suspecting neighbors or family members or strangers in public spaces. The forces want to torment others and do this by being hostile and aggressive. The possessed have vicious personalities, are morally vicious, belligerent, and unethical, and see the world differently. Ultimately, the goal is to make the victims whom the possessed abuses, to lose hope and faith in God. Without a connection to God and the church, victims of abuse can, and, often do, succumb to suicide because they see no way out. That is why some people give up, because they can't put some distance between themselves and their spiritual or physical abuser. Despair in the victim, resulting from the torment by the demonic abuser is the ultimate goal of the dark forces, and Satan opposes God's people.

Not all mental illnesses are a result of demonic influence; and not all demonic influence is total possession. Sometimes, instead of being internal, the dark forces are in the surrounding environment, i.e., in a living space at home like their livingrooms or bedrooms. People can be sensitive or open, mentally, to the spiritual world surrounding them and occasionally be swayed by suggestion from such an outside force. A person may think that an exterior voice is speaking to them, telling them things from the surrounding environment. Often, this spiritual influence does not enter the human being's brain or mind, but the human can intercept it. The goal of the source of the voice is to torment, accuse, and destroy the hope of the victim—for when hope is gone, all is lost. The voice may consist of a message, thought or repetitious thoughts, that condemn the victim repeatably. Often the voice/thought will swear at the victim and call them names. It will also communicate obscenities about other people the victim knows, showing strong hatred. All of these things are tortuous for the victim who hears this, and it causes severe distress. Additional stresses, such as being outdoors in extreme summer heat or being hungry with low blood sugars can exacerbate the condition, leading to desperation or angry fits.

Sometimes humans are not aware of something being an outside force and they may think the intruding thoughts are their own, coming from their own thinking. Though it's possible some thoughts will originate from within oneself, this isn't always the case. Demons, evil spirits, will speak into the mind of the victims either with or without their own knowledge. The damage can be immense. Along with prayer, this is where anti-psychotic medication comes in. I go into detail in my previous work, *Voices in the Rain: Meaning in Psychosis*[9] where I state that as illicit, recreational drugs such as LSD or marijuana change the brain chemistry to allow an influence of the demonic, opening the mind to the spiritual realm (i.e., voices)—the psychiatric medications, such as risperidone and Clozapine, can desensitize a person from the spiritual realm by acting on the same brain processes where the opening occurs, only in reverse. Usually, though, medication is only a partial help and it depends upon each individual case. Generally speaking, a person with mental illness will be a lot worse off if he or she doesn't take any medicine or when there are no spiritual interventions that a religious faith and faith community contributes.

So along with medication, prayer is our weapon. We pray to shield ourselves from such spiritual abuse because prayer directed to God, through Jesus Christ, can offer protection. Not many of us have the power to exorcise someone we know who is totally possessed, be it a neighbor or relative.

9. Murphy, *Voices in the Rain*, 177–78.

A person would need to seek God's help and pray over it, asking Jesus to intervene. We also need to clear away the dark forces from around us, in our livingrooms, bedrooms, etc. But the complete exorcism of the neighbor or relative is ultimately God's work and we can't expect to do it ourselves, though we mustn't lose hope. There is a great risk of being attacked, ourselves, by spiritual forces if we try to exorcise someone—which we should not take lightly. Roman Catholic priests may be some of the best people to assist in this situation.[10] God has given some individuals the ability to cast out demons, e.g., certain psychiatrists or religious leaders like pastors or priests, but not many. Here is a biblical example of such people, those among Jesus's followers:

And he called the twelve [Apostles] and began to send them out two by two, and gave them authority over the unclean spirits . . . And they cast out many demons and anointed with oil many who were sick and healed them. Mark 8:7, 13 (ESV).

When a mentally ill person may suspect they have a demon (or demons) inside of themselves the best action to take is to become involved with a Christian community, attend weekly worship services, and take psychiatric medication. But along with this is saying a prayer of deliverance stating that Jesus Christ has authority over all things in heaven and on earth (Matt 28:18) and asking Jesus to remove the demons from within themselves: *Jesus, by your power and authority, please expel the demons out of me, and fill me with the Holy Spirit. Put a shield around me and protect me by your power and authority.* Such a prayer of deliverance might be needed more than once during a lifetime because the person with mental illness can be susceptible to continuous spiritual influences over the course of their entire lifetime.

❖ ❖ ❖

Church friends Randy Hausler and his wife, Peg Hausler, were missionaries to Haiti. They provided the following responses to my questionnaire:[11] This section is particularly relevant for providing the context of deprivation that developing countries are challenged with. With few resources available to treat mental illness in Haiti, the excerpt below reveals how many who have mental illness there suffer because of a lack of resources for treatment and care. We in the developed nations have a wealth of resources and therefore it is imperative to use wisdom with the best rationality and thoughtfulness in how our resources are to be used for the utmost good and not for ill. Ideally,

10. Amorth, *An Exorcist Explains*, 17.

11. Randy and Peg Hausler, email to author, 9/15/2018.

we, the richer nations, could offer material resources and some healthcare personnel and religious support to countries like Haiti.

Randy and Peg Hausler: Here are the answers you requested. However, I would preface the answers with the fact that the conditions in Haiti are difficult to describe. The overwhelming need to tend to basic necessities like food, water and clothing, are consuming—meaning that medical care (both physical and mental) often go without a response. People die of very basic things that would not happen in this country: there is often no treatment for things like blood pressure and diabetes because that takes monitoring. There are no resources for monitoring since people often do not have access to regular medical care. To discuss mental health in a country so deprived of basic resources is difficult because mental health also takes ongoing treatment: counseling and/or medicine. Thus, most mental illness simply goes untreated. It is a sad reality.

We did a sabbatical in Haiti for three months in 2001 but have returned for visits more than a dozen times. Those trips generally lasted about one week. While there we were charged to support the mission of the Haitian-American Friendship Foundation. They have an on-site school on their property as well as a dental and medical clinic. They partner with Haitians in the Central Plateau of Haiti through academic, vocational, and theological education to enrich the lives spiritually, economically, and socially—all to the glory of God. Duties varied widely during our visits. It might include teaching classes at the school, making supply runs to a nearby village, assisting with clinics, and helping the on-site missionaries in any way possible.

In the very rural areas that we generally stayed in mental illness went relatively undiagnosed. The people do not have financial resources to travel to cities to get any assistance, diagnosis or medications. Since voodoo is fairly prevalent, sometimes people would think that the person was *possessed*. But generally, there is so much strife and poverty where we stayed that people with mental illness simply experienced tremendous isolation and were left to fend for themselves. Generally, a person with mental illness presented (physically) as very unkept. Without running water in most homes, even getting clean via a trip to a working pump or a river to rinse off takes effort.

The hospitals provide very basic acute care for physical ailments. There really isn't any clinic that we ever saw that was for treating those with mental illness. It isn't a stretch to say that there really aren't any specialty clinics for mentally ill patients. When severe depression, for example, presents in a patient, they might try to provide food or clothing. However, there is no attempt to connect with counseling (doesn't exist) or medications (too expensive).

Those that are mentally or physically ill are generally not treated as outcasts. The culture is for families to care for their own. Communities expect that families will care for their own members. There are barely vocabulary words in the creole language to discuss mental health in Haiti. Typically, there is no spectrum discussed. They only think about mental illness in severe terms and call the person "crazy." The challenge in Haiti—and in the majority of developing countries—is that access to mental health care is extremely limited. As recently as 2012, in Haiti, there were just five psychiatrists and one neurologist for a population of 10 million. We cannot fathom the lack of resources. [End of Hauslers' response.]

❖ ❖ ❖

Rev. Carl Beyerhelm and his wife, Beatrice (Bea) Beyerhelm, and their family were in Tanganyika/Tanzania from 1955–1964. Carl was a parish pastor and then a seminary professor and Bea was a mother, teacher of women's classes in sewing, cooking, and leadership especially at the seminary. They lived primarily in rural areas, not the city. They were under the Board of Missions for the Evangelical Lutheran Church in American (ELCA). Bea provided the following responses to my questionnaire.[12]

Bea Beyerhelm: In the rural area families tried to just keep their mentally ill family members out of sight, but took care of them. In the cities, the mentally ill tended to become homeless street people and beggars. If they weren't violent, they were tolerated. What we mostly saw or heard about was connected to evil spirits or ancestors who were angry about something and so brought illness (not identified as mental) or misfortune or death to the family. The native family response was to isolate the ill person, appease the ancestors with offerings, or to consult with a native medicine man. I don't think they ever saw it as a medical problem. It was a relational problem.

There was some fear that somehow the *bad luck* of the ill would spread and people were isolated and avoided, even shunned or feared. As far as I know there was no specific education or treatment on a Western model. There was no real help or medication or care. That was in the 1960s and it may be different now.

An experience was told to me by a woman. One night her family heard birds on their roof and she believed the birds would bring death. She woke up her family and they knelt in prayer for safety. She told me, "I know you don't believe in the spirits, but we know Jesus is stronger and will help us." [End of comments by Bea Beyerhelm]

12. Bea Beyerhelm, email to author, 7/25/2018.

❖ ❖ ❖

My church friend Dr. Cecilia Norris (Medical Director, Iowa City Free Medical & Dental Clinic), did four one-week trips over a period of four years in Guatemala with a group from Saint Andrew Presbyterian Church, Iowa City, Iowa.

Dr. Cecilia Norris: My primary responsibilities and areas of work were coordinating medical clinics for people who usually couldn't see a doctor. I saw those patients and provided the medical care I could. In answer to the question of what were my impressions regarding native people who had a mental illness and what were the symptoms or behaviors they displayed: I saw a lot of people with depression and anxiety and it was difficult to tell how much stemmed from their stressful living conditions, poor nutrition, and lack of preventive health care. Most of the symptoms were physical ones, especially pain, i.e., headaches, abdominal pain, and musculoskeletal pain. There were several people with difficulty sleeping, low mood and, low energy. In answer to the question: What were the ill person's beliefs and interpretations regarding the symptoms, the ones I was able to communicate with usually felt that their symptoms were from their difficult life. The short duration of visits made it difficult to delve very deep into this. What did people do to combat mental illness? Most of them used prayer.

Marcia Murphy: What efforts were made to treat the mentally ill person?

Dr. Cecilia Norris: There were not any facilities available and people could not afford treatment at the rural locations I visited. There were no therapists or psychiatrists in the area so people would have had to travel several hours in order to see a qualified provider. This was prohibitively expensive for most people (both cost to travel to other locations and time off of work for appointments). The medications were only limitedly available when medical missionary groups came to bring them. The one doctor I worked mostly recommended prayers and he tried to alleviate physical symptoms but was not able to provide long-term therapy or counseling.

Question: Were the mentally ill treated as outcasts or integrated within families and the communities? The people I saw were integrated within their families but that may have been a select population because many of the mentally ill would need help to get a clinic. The families generally tried to be supportive but were struggling themselves as a family member with mental illness often could not help with the necessary tasks in the home.[13][End of Dr. Cecilia Norris's comments]

13. Cecilia Norris, MD, email to author, 8/13/2018.

❖ ❖ ❖

Lynn Fogleman, MD, and his wife, Sharon Fogleman, MD, are Family Physicians and worked in a hospital, and then in Community Health Training in Kenya (1987–1997) and Southeast Kentucky (1997–2011) under the General Board of Global Ministries. Then in South Sudan/Uganda (2012–2016) and Lynn, alone (to 2018) under TMS Global.

Dr. Sharon Fogleman: Most of the anti-social behaviors evident in Kenya were related to bipolar illness and schizophrenia. Their families suffered as these problems were often attributed to demon-possession or bewitching. Many were on the streets and ended up being abused and addicted to alcohol to cover symptoms. In South Sudan, the trauma of life with war and its consequences led to increased domestic violence and suicide, as well as alcohol abuse and HIV. Many felt hopeless and believed there was no treatment or hope available. Unfortunately, seizure disorders were lumped into the same category as mental illness and families/individuals viewed them together. But health education also was well-received, that indeed Jesus was a healing power and medications could help. Families definitely suffered the consequences of fear of such illness by the community. Thankfully the church and community were open to seeing the people as a part of them when they were not violent.

Unfortunately, there was inadequate healthcare for the mentally ill. In Kenya more psychiatric nurses were being trained, although psychiatrists were very few in number. There was a mental health hospital in Nairobi, but often the acute psychosis was treated in our hospital with strong meds, and restraints for the violent. In South Sudan, most of the care was community-based with very few mental health staff. In Yei, there was one psychiatric nurse and only one psychiatrist in the whole country prior to the migration of refugees in 2016. Meds were available but expensive for most patients and families. Expansion of mental health services in most African countries is much needed and beneficial to the people. [End of Dr. Sharon Fogleman's comments]

❖ ❖ ❖

Elizabeth Ebot lived in Cameroon, her native land, which is situated in the West-Central part of Africa. She is not a missionary—she lived there from birth to age seventeen, and was in school.

Elizabeth Ebot: My impressions regarding native people with mental illness was extreme fear held by the community in which the mentally ill lived; and this was because they (the mentally ill) were considered dangerous who could cause harm to those around them. Most often, unfortunately, they just roamed around homeless and unkept. If at all, they received treatment, it was from native doctors who used harsh methods such as beatings. They believed beating the mentally ill persons somewhat cured them.

Family members/friends always thought mental illness most often was brought on by oneself or by the family of the mentally ill person, e.g., abusing drugs, participating in occult practices, family curses etc. The effect on both the family and the ill person was detrimental. People didn't get married into such families for fear of bringing forth children who could have a mental illness also. I wouldn't say much was done back then to combat mental illness. But what I say is that with more and more people becoming Christians it has opened up a new way to combat stress, anxiety and other supports of mental health through the belief in God. The more people have turned to God through faith, the more their well-being has improved.

Because the government healthcare (clinics/hospitals) is too expensive for most people, the mentally ill person ends up being treated by native doctors. As I said previously, they use very harsh forms of treatments like beatings. They also administer native drugs or natural substances made from leaves etc. To the best of my knowledge, most mentally ill persons are treated as outcasts. They generally roam the streets and are homeless; they aren't integrated within their families.[14]

The person who provided treatment for me for nearly twenty-five years in the form of a psychiatric professional—someone who knows me very well—said the following:

"Your psychosis, i.e., voices of the demons or devil, was like the temptation of Jesus when Jesus encountered the devil in the wilderness."[15] Jesus heard the devil speaking to him. It was a time of trial and suffering, spiritual warfare, fighting, and clinging to God and God's word, in Holy scripture. And Christ defeated the devil. Unfortunately, many people with mental illness do not survive such trauma.

William James, American philosopher and psychologist, wrote that we can understand something more distinctly by seeing it in exaggerated form.[16] My experience of being under an extreme demonic attack going so far as a threat on my life, showed how the dark forces that surround us, often unaware, can appear audibly in a sensitive person's hearing; what Western psychiatry has termed as hallucinations. Many thought disorders are akin to this phenomenon as well.

14. Elizabeth Ebot, email to author, 9/27/2018.

15. Dr. Russell Noyes Jr., email to author, 2000.

16. James, *Religious Experience*, 39, 45.

My psychotic break in my early adult years was similar to a near-death experience (NDE) in the sense that I was fighting for my life—psychologically and physically—with no guarantee of success. It was only by the grace of God that I survived. For some unknown reason, the Lord had sympathy for my plight and reached out in the voice in the rain. When oppressed by the demonic forces, God, in his mercy, intervened and saved me, body and soul.

There is another example of God intervening to save someone. In Bruce Greyson's *After: A Doctor Explores What Near-Death Experiences Reveal about Life and Beyond,* a young man named Peter, in a psychotic episode, jumped from his dorm roof when in the throes of a psychotic break, obeying demonic voices; but as he fell, he heard what he believed was the voice of God who told him he didn't want Peter to die. Peter survived that fall with only some broken bones, living to tell about it.[17] Bruce Greyson wrote that he doesn't believe that there is a relationship between mental illness and near-death experiences,[18] but I don't agree. I think some people have death-rebirth experiences with psychosis like I did. With my belief in the voice in the rain, my life was transformed in a positive, new direction.

In Allan Kellehear's book, *Experiences Near Death*, he states that people have many crises over the course of their lives, e.g., illness, divorce, death of loved ones, job loss, disappointments, failures, natural disasters, accidents, assaults on our character or physical well-being, etc. These are experiences where we die a little bit (or completely) to an old self and are re-born anew into a new outlook on the scope of things, including, but not limited to, our religious outlook.[19]

The near-death experience Kellehear, as a sociologist, is talking about, may also involve some instances of severe mental illness which can be considered as another form of dying-to-self-phenomena. I agree with Kellehear that sometimes a crisis will tragically destroy various aspects of a person, allowing no opportunity for renewal or restoration. And that is why the church which consists of the body of Christ, is so vitally important. Without them, for example, I would not have made it.

I point to the need to integrate spiritual and medical modalities to improve recovery outcomes and the quality of life for the ill. However, a great challenge in international settings is not only socioeconomic difficulties—including lack of resources which hinder access to psychiatric care and treatments—but the complex systemic corruptions in structures of government that intercept and/or block desperately needed aid intended for the populace.

17. Greyson, *After*, 77–78.
18. Greyson, *After*, 88–89.
19. Kellehear, *Experiences Near Death*, 163–4.

Chapter 5

Healing Through Immersion

Prayer, Water, Aesthetics, Music, and Sacraments

Now I would like to talk about the various ways I have found healing. Healing from not just physical injury or illness; but, also, emotional and incorporeal (non-physical) healing for mental and spiritual health. There are some basic things I do daily and some are done weekly or monthly.

First of all, if I didn't start my day with scripture reading and prayer, I'd be a total mess for the rest of the day. Prayer, especially, is vital for my mental health. Besides morning prayer, I also say brief prayers interspersed throughout the day and a short prayer at bedtime which usually helps me sleep better.

The University of Minnesota's Earl E. Bakken's Center for Spirituality and Healing spokesperson, the Rev. Catherine Duncan, BCC, has this to say about prayer:

> Prayer has a very personal meaning arising from an individual's religious background or spiritual practice. For some, prayer will mean specific sacred words; for others, it may be a more informal talking or listening to God or a higher power. The word "prayer" comes from the Latin *precarius*, which means "obtained by begging, to entreat." Prayer is rooted in the belief that there is a power greater than oneself that can influence one's life. It is the act of raising hearts and minds to God or a higher power. There is no one set way to pray. Forms include spoken prayers, silent

prayers, and prayers of the mind, the heart, and union with God. Prayers may be directed (e.g., prayers for specific things) or non-directed, with no specific outcome in mind.[1]

The Rev. Dr. Timothy Keller's video, Primacy of Prayer, says that we need to understand how vital our daily personal prayer life is for everyday existence.[2] As I have mentioned, I have personally found that my day goes a lot better if I start it with prayer, preceded by scripture reading. Asking God for guidance and blessing, direction for my projects, and interceding for others—there is endless variety for what people might find personally helpful. Since God is our Creator, how foolish it would be to leave out God. There is no greater method than laying the groundwork of daily morning prayer for a more successful and meaningful existence. Alessandro DiSanto states in the spiritual resource, Grotto, that there are several ways prayer can be helpful: It helps us combat addictions and resist temptations; makes us more resilient to stress; improves overall physical and emotional health.[3]

Phil Cary states: I think prayer is a form of seeking, a way of asking God for what you need, the way a child asks a good father. My objection is to turning it into a technique—as if you were guaranteed to get what you want if only you use the technique right. That bypasses the wisdom of God, who knows what is good for us better than we do. It turns prayer from a personal relationship (one person asking another for help) into a kind of machinery (push the right button and you'll get what you want.)[4] [End of Phil Cary on prayer.]

Another immersion that promotes healing involves water. In The History of Psychiatry, Shorter states that ever since ancient times, water has been utilized in a therapeutic way.[5] He describes how there was a practice of using spas for psychiatric illnesses ever since the eighteenth century.[6]

Ever since my youth I have enjoyed swimming, mostly in public pools. This has been something that has contributed joy in my life as well as promoted my physical health. My parents saw to it that their children had lessons, I am grateful for that. And even though I almost drowned once in the deep end (and the swimming instructor jumped in to save me), I have loved everything about swimming: the way the sun is reflected from the water; the splashing and pounding of feet against the water when swim teams are

1. Duncan, Prayer, para 1–3.
2. Keller, Primacy of Prayer, 4/18/2018.
3. DiSanto, Keep the Faith, Prayer, para 1–3.
4. Phil Cary, email to author, 9/6/2021.
5. Shorter, History of Psychiatry, 119.
6. Shorter, History of Psychiatry, 23–24, 119–20.

working out. Usually, there is a friendly greeting from other participants which creates an informal swim social club where you aren't judged by the clothes you wear or your hair style because everyone is wearing a swimsuit and cap on the head. There are colorful kickboards and pull buoys—good things for strengthening and firming up the muscles. A person can take the lap swimming very seriously and strenuously, going very fast; or do what I do—see the act of being in the water and movement as type of meditation and almost of prayer where God's healing takes place.

I injured my head a few years ago from a fall and, later, also had Basel cell cancer removal surgery in another spot on my forehead. After the incisions were completely healed, being in a swimming pool helped me to feel better, especially swimming underwater. Walking in the water and swimming also helped in the process of healing my joint and muscle pain from other conditions. For me, being in the water is also mentally and emotionally healing, e.g., meditative, calming, peaceful. Once I felt it was the Kingdom of Heaven while floating on my back and looking straight up. And even though I only saw the building's ceiling—it still felt blissful. For those for whom a swimming pool is not accessible—either for financial reasons, or other reasons, e.g., no pool available in their city—a nice long bath or shower in one's own home can provide the same calming and spiritually cleansing opportunity for healing which can be done every day.

So, I have found that water-based exercise improves my mental health; it generally improves my mood and lessens depression. I, personally, enjoy water-based exercise more than on land. I can exercise longer in water than on land without increased effort or severe joint or muscle pain. But some people enjoy land exercises like walking outdoors. I have a senior church friend named Myrna who shared her experiences with me on the benefits of walking, and gave me permission to include them here.

> Having married someone five and a half years younger than myself, I felt I'd better stay fit so people didn't say, "Why'd he marry that old woman?" That's just a joke but partly true, I think. I've been active since my youth and have maintained exercising in one form or another all my life. Now, it is for my soul as well as my body. This morning I started out at 5:40 and walked for about an hour and a half depending on how much garbage there is because I pick up the litter as I go. I love it! It's my time to pray, sing, recite scripture, and plan the day. Also, I enjoy the birds singing, the rabbits out to catch the morning sun, and the deer walking through the woods: all God's creatures. I pray for their safe day as well as the people that I pass, either walking,

running, or on bikes. I insist on greeting all I meet with Good Morning! Makes me feel good. A great way to start the day.[7]

I have also discovered the benefits of yarncrafts. Aesthetically, I enjoy the many colors of the yarn and love the tactile pleasures of feeling the yarn and needles or hooks in my hands and fingers; and I find joy in the finished product. I've knitted and crocheted, creating winter scarves and blankets, and hope to learn more. Some of the benefits I've found are that it improves my mood and cognition, and helps me to be more logical and rational. Blogger and author Kathryn Vercillo is an expert in the area of using crafting to heal, having researched the topic extensively for her book, *Crochet Saved My Life*. She states that:

> Yarn heals. Whether you prefer needles or hooks or a combination of both, crafting can soothe your body and mend your mind. Anecdotal evidence has shown this for decades and new research confirms it with science. The benefits people report are seemingly endless. Here are the top ten yarncrafting, i.e., knitting and crocheting, health benefits: Relieves depression; helps to reduces anxiety; builds self-esteem; may reduce or postpone dementia; helps with insomnia. [The] relaxation reduces irritability and restlessness; can be used as prayer or with prayer; builds community [when done with others]; helps with grief processing; reduces stress.[8]

In the WebMD article, *Brain Exercises May Delay Memory Loss*, it states that engaging in activities that exercise the brain, like reading and even knitting, may delay or prevent memory loss, researchers report. In a new study reading magazines, knitting and quilting, and social activities in midlife cut the risk that people would develop memory loss in their 70s or 80s by more than one-third. And if you've already turned 70 or 80, it's not too late to benefit from exercises that tax the brain, says researcher Yonas Geda, MD, a neuropsychiatrist at the Mayo Clinic in Rochester, Minn. In later years, reading books, playing games, and doing craft activities lowered the chance of memory loss by about one-third, the study shows.[9]

Here, again, is Myrna:

> I didn't knit until after college and I was teaching in Amman, Jordan at the Girls' School. The friends I made were knitting beautiful sweaters and I was interested in learning. They did a

---

7. Myrna Farraj, email to author, 6/08/2021.

8. Vercillo, *10 Benefits Yarncrafting*, para 1–10.

9. Laino, *Brain Exercises*, lines 1–8.

good job teaching me. I've taught quite a number of people to knit—which is fun for me. Right now, I'm in two knitting groups that meet for fun and support. One's the Prayer Shawl group and the other is just a knitting group in general with mostly people from church. As for crocheting, I think I was curious and got a book to follow— made myself an orange hat. Wrong color for me is the joke. But I don't enjoy crocheting like knitting so I stick to knitting. This year I'm 87. I'm giving myself 10 more years and that seems too short, but I'll try to fill them wisely.[10]

Generally speaking, what I call *aesthetics therapy*, in a psychological sense, and self-applied, is something I use to try to feel better. I believe being surrounded by beauty in the home, neighborhood, workplace, or city, can be uplifting for the mood and restorative for the soul. This idea brought with it the question of beauty—what it is—whether it is an objective reality or just subjective, according to individual taste. One area Phil Cary is an expert in—philosophy—discusses this very question, so I asked for his opinion.

I explained my question to Phil Cary: You have said that beauty is an absolute. You said *everyone* should be able to see beauty. I see no options there for subjective opinions of what beauty consists of. I would guess that there are probably two camps in opposite corners on this issue.

Phil Cary: Yes, there are two camps—and more—when it comes to beauty. I'm in the camp that goes back to Plato, thinking that beauty is a reality independent of our minds, which means we can be wrong about it, miss it, fail to perceive it—but by the same token, we can learn to see it better, grow in our understanding of it, become more skillful and adept at it. Here's why: I think as you grow more skillful you perceive things more accurately, and that perceiving the beauty of a particular kind of music (Mozart, Jazz) is a skill. Skills are learned: you *learn* to hear the beauty in Mozart or see the beauty in a great novel. All skills, like all learning, involve recognizing the difference between perceiving well and perceiving badly—otherwise there would be no difference between learning and not learning. So, if perceiving the beauty of something requires skill and learning, then beauty must be a reality independent of our minds. For if it were entirely dependent on our minds or feelings, then we couldn't be wrong about it. That's the flip side: if you can't be wrong about it, then you can't learn it, for then there is no difference between getting it wrong and getting it right, no difference between having learned and not having learned. And I think it's obvious that we can *learn* to perceive the beauty of Mozart's music. This is not just growing to like it. It's learning to perceive something real. Our life is richer

---

10. Myrna Farraj, email to author, 6/7/2021.

after learning to perceive this particular beauty, not just because it has more pleasure in it (which of course it does) but because we know something about the reality outside of us that we didn't know before. We're in contact with more of the reality that God has created. For behind the music making of Mozart is the creativity of God. A Mozart symphony is a gift of God to the world. It is God's creation, not just Mozart's, for God created Mozart, his mind and skill and works. There is no good and beautiful and real thing that is not God's creation.[11]

Marcia Murphy: But then again, all kinds of people end up getting married and having offspring—in fact, I would argue most of them are homely or unattractive. So, what is it people love if it isn't some kind of beauty—non-Hollywood-style? This would stand as evidence against absolute beauty and lean toward subjective tastes.

Phil Cary: The classical answer to that seems to me to be right: There is such a thing as beauty of soul, which is a moral quality, consisting of virtues like kindness, generosity, fidelity. That's the kind of beauty that is most important to seek in a mate. If you marry someone morally ugly, you get heartache, infidelity, abuse.[12] [End of Phil Cary's comments on beauty]

I also believe that color is a healing influence. Color is all around us. Even for those legally blind, color comes to them in their dreams. We can decorate our homes or visit art galleries to enrich our mental health because artwork, done by both the masters and amateurs, can teach, lift up, or exemplify great truths. There are many ways artwork affects us. An acquaintance from church, professional artist Cary Maassen, shared his thoughts on the value of great artwork and how artwork affects us. I share his thoughts below to show the healing effects of aesthetics through art and its role in uplifting and teaching us.

Cary Maassen (on concerning the essence of the fine arts): All my adult life people have challenged with: "What's so special about Picasso, all he does is that abstract junk!" But if one looks in depth at that junk and studies it as a treatise, they will encounter significant insight. Not every piece he did will be of interest to every person and not every piece he did is a masterpiece but neither is every piece written by Shakespeare of interest to everyone. The insight is still inherent in his works. One Picasso that can be used as an example is *Guernica*. If one piece can explain all the intricacies of the horrors of war it must be Guernica. If one contemplates all the elements of this painting, they will probably not want to hang it where they will have to constantly be reminded of the atrocities of war. The art world is replete with

11. Phil Cary, email to author, 11/19/2020.
12. Phil Cary, email to author, 11/19/2020.

many similar revelations, especially in religious artwork. How could anyone enjoy the crown of thorns and the crucifixion? Good artwork is meant to reveal, teach, illuminate! Is it not those *I see* moments that broaden our understanding of human existence that lift us up? Then we can flip the coin over and look at love and compassion in the same light of understanding![13]

Cary Maassen continues: It is true as you say that art can lift up. But I would point out that we also learn by negative example to value what is true and beautiful. For example, one can learn the value of love and goodwill when seeing a painting of a horrible battle field and how awful violence and strife are, thereby pushing us to strive for peace and beauty. So, negative, dark, artwork also can teach. I would not discount them. Just as long as they are not profane or obscene. Sadness has its teaching value and we learn from the sadness in art as well as the sunshine. Look at the Bible, it is full of negative examples to teach us: the book of Lamentations is a good example. And look at Christ in the crucifixion—a most horrible situation which God uses for our redemption.[14] [End of Cary Maassen's comments.]

Another area of aesthetics is music. I find healing from listening to music, whether in-person at church; or through my computer, previously recorded music. I do not have many opportunities for live music, usually. There have been a lot of academics and health care professions studying music's therapeutic effects. Many thoughtful individuals state that music has therapeutic qualities—which has long been known.[15]

Lyle Juracek, Instructional Service Specialist and Dance Musician, describes what, for him, is the healing power of music or mental health with music. He says:

> Music is an interesting art. We know we hear it and we know we feel it. And, especially, if you are a part of a church or quietly relaxing at home, you are aware that your spirit's presence is being affected. By listening quietly and letting yourself be receptive to the sound that a voice, an instrument, or a symphony make, it is indeed affecting your being. Does music make you happy or sad? Yes, it has the power to elate you and stir you up. And, it can carry deep into yourself and bring images of melancholy and reflection. Music is interesting in that it can participate as a close friend or as a passive acquaintance. Because it is just there, it can possess you—it can give you ideas for creativity and it can transcend those ideas into a structure that becomes a composition. Music therapists use it as a healing agent through the use

13. Cary Maassen, email to author, 4/18/2021.

14. Cary Maassen, email to author, 4/18/2021.

15. Young-Mason, "Music Therapy," 153–4.

of its melodic and rhythmic motion, helping the spirit accept things as they are, and then, to move on.[16]

And now I will turn to healing through a Christian practice known as the Holy Eucharist, a sacrament. My understanding of the Eucharist, i.e., the bread and wine (or juice) would be closer to medieval Catholicism than a modern-day Baptist ordinance, but only that the body and blood of Christ is Christ's presence for me in a spiritual way. And by taking part in this physical sacrament of eating the bread and drinking the wine (or juice) which is something external to myself, Christ comes inside of me, and I am one with Christ. As it is written in John 15: 4–5 (ESV): *Abide in me, and I in you. As the branch cannot bear fruit by itself, unless it abides in the vine, neither can you, unless you abide in me. I am the vine; you are the branches. Whoever abides in me and I in him, he it is that bears much fruit, for apart from me you can do nothing.* In that moment I am connected with Christ the myriad sinful ways of my past are forgiven; and though my sinful ways may resume or persist in the future, at least in the moment of consuming the Eucharist, I am holy and one with Christ; Christ in me. This practice of holy communion is a step toward wholeness and, subsequently, sanity as well. In past years, when I went without the sacraments, I was, I believe, driven insane, and became spiritually dead—largely cut off from God, the life-giving source.

On our connection with Christ in Ephesians 2:1–10 (ESV) says:

> And you were dead in the trespasses and sins in which you once walked, following the course of this world, following the prince of the power of the air, the spirit that is now at work in the sons of disobedience—among whom we all once lived in the passions of our flesh, carrying out the desires of the body and the mind, and were by nature children of wrath, like the rest of mankind. But God, being rich in mercy, because of the great love with which he loved us, even when we were dead in our trespasses, made us alive together with Christ—by grace you have been saved— and raised us up with him and seated us with him in the heavenly places in Christ Jesus, so that in the coming ages he might show the immeasurable riches of his grace in kindness toward us in Christ Jesus.

I know this experientially; I know in my heart that it is true. I have felt and experienced the difference of *before* and *after* of the taking of the Eucharist. And no amount of a liberal pastor's preaching, claiming my understanding of the Eucharist is just magical thinking or superstitious, will

---

16. Lyle Juracek, essay communication to author, June 3, 2021.

ever change my mind. It is more than symbolic or a sign because my mental health is dependent upon this union with Christ along with the waters of baptism and the reading of scripture. *And I believe that the further one strays from these exact things mental health deteriorates in the degree or proportion of the separation.* Therefore, Christianity is a saving faith in more ways than one, as it has been demonstrated throughout the centuries: *It's either Christ or madness.* Human beings are all living on a spectrum showing degrees of sanity and madness. No one is perfectly sane, but there are degrees of sanity. And since God is the life-giving force, for an individual to choose to be willingly cut off from God is the ultimate suicidal insanity.

Conclusion

Abundant Life

I came that they may have life and have it abundantly.

John 10:10b (ESV)

When I was a little girl, a mere toddler of nearly three years, I would run up to my mother on my chubby legs and tug on her apron: "Mommy, church?? *Church??!!*

"No, dear, not today," my mother would say (a bit impatient because I did this several times a week): "Sunday—Sunday, we will go to church!"

My eyes cast down, I would slowly back away. *Not today. But I want to see Jesus.*

How I loved the church with the hymns, the singing choirs, the lighted candles. People of all ages all dressed up and bowing their heads in prayer. The stillness and peace, God's presence. Joy would fill my heart and my innocent, young life had meaning.

❖ ❖ ❖

Spirituality does not replace medicine; however, it is a strong influence for positive health outcomes, not just physically, but emotionally, mentally, and spiritually. Sometimes God allows or even sends physical illness in order to restore us in other ways. We all know people who were changed for the better by a physical illness or catastrophe. Stories of transformation fill the Best Seller lists.

I asked Phil Cary the following: Some people think that humans can't learn to change bad behavior to become better humans. But then we would not have Christian formation in churches or schools. And there would be no point in parents disciplining their children, right?

Phil Cary responded: We change all the time. It's just that changing for the better is much harder than changing for the worse. The disagreement, I suppose, is about *how* hard it is, and how far we can change. It's a lot like recovering from physical wounds. We don't always fully recover.[1] [End of Phil Cary's comments on change.]

I believe that to improve both brain and mental health there are some steps people can take. Treatments such as medication and psychotherapy are important. Attending religious services once a week as well as reading scripture on a regular basis along with Christian education classes can help instill good character. Forming meaningful relationships with others in a religious community is helpful. Along with medications to help combat acute psychotic symptoms, it is psychologically necessary for growth to occur in positive spiritual formation; and along with this, one needs to eliminate any negative traits developed in early life. In order to make some personal changes I, personally, found I had to revisit all those dark emotions and states of being, coming out victorious on the other side into the new realm of health, leaving those old traits behind. Transformation can, therefore, be quite painful as with the change from darkness to light. However, the trauma involved with transformation is not only for the benefit of oneself, it also benefits others in our social group and community at large.

With a well-rounded development of the personality a human can experience integrity of mind which includes the thinking inherent therein. C.S. Lewis explained that paradoxically, it begins with denial of the self to reach a higher good comprised of a life centered on God. Lewis stated that the more we focus on ourselves in a self-centered and selfish way the more we find ruin. But when we deny ourselves in a kind of death and do things with God's purposes in mind, we find a new self. And as the human personality becomes more and more developed into perfection, each human being becomes remarkable and more distinct one from another. The new personality is Christ in us—but in our own unique selves—and thus the evolving, unique holistic personalities are a result of our union with Christ.[2]

What is to be Done?

Everything, then, begins in the home.

---

1. Phil Cary, email to author, 5/27/21.
2. Lewis, *Mere Christianity*, Audio Recording, March, 21, 1944.

How we are treated by parents and siblings, and how we treat them, is the basic foundation. Do we have pure hearts in relationships, good morals, and respect for others? Are we teachable, i.e., able to receive instruction, willing to follow directions? Do we revere God and strive to obey his commandments? And revere life, simply, itself, doing no harm to ourselves or to others? Do we love as Christ loves, and give of ourselves for the benefit of the family as a whole, the church, and broader community?

As I mentioned earlier, a well-established phenomenon called the Pygmalion Effect[3] should be taught in all medical schools which would include psychiatry rotations since this effect has a powerful place in the therapeutic relationship between healthcare provider and patient. This far-reaching effect is also applicable to other areas of academia as well as in *any* social environment—wherever there is human interaction of any kind. Unfortunately, we can be caught off guard in any casual encounter.

Peter Kreeft, a Roman Catholic professor who discusses ethics and moral thought, said that according to him some major questions in life are as follows: *What is being good? What is being successful? What is the meaning of life?*[4] He says that ethics is about good behavior and the kind of person we are supposed to be. And why should we be good people? What is life's purpose, the point of life? Some believe it is obtaining success—assuming life has some point. However, in modern culture, there is no goal or end for life, no objective. These issues are ignored.[5]

Phil Cary: What the whole Western tradition from Plato onwards agrees about is that the chief end of man, the ultimate goal, is happiness (also known as beatitude or felicity). Augustine adds: this is what philosophy is all about, because philosophy is the pursuit of wisdom, and to attain divine wisdom is happiness. So, it's really important to understand that "happiness" does not designate a feeling, though it can certainly include feelings (Aristotle and Augustine and Aquinas think it does). What it designates, I'd say, is "true success in life, whatever that might be." I say all this because Happiness is arguably the key concept in Western philosophy (Augustine actually says as much), so if you treat happiness as if it were only a feeling, nothing more, then you'll misunderstand Aristotle and just about every other philosopher in the West. But the flip side is this: it does not mean happiness doesn't feel good. Of course, happiness feels good. But it's not just a feeling. Think of the happiness of a great musician playing great music beautifully. It feels good, but it's more than just a feeling: it's an activity that

---

3. Duquesne University, *"Pygmalion"* lines 1–4.
4. Kreeft, *Ethics: History of Moral Thought,* audio CD.
5. Kreeft, *Ethics: History of Moral Thought,* audio CD.

fulfills his identity as a musician. So also, human happiness is the activity (e.g., glorifying God and enjoying him forever) that fulfills human nature most deeply and completely.[6] [End of Phil Cary]

I ask, what is the summum bonum, the ultimate end in life? In biblical text, at the end of the book of Ecclesiastes it states that the meaning of life is to *fear God and keep his commandments.* Eccles 12:12 (ESV). Kreeft states that modern culture's philosophy says that *life is meaningless, so why care? There is nothing worth doing*—which is moral insanity. *Life means nothing.* Which leads us to humans' most basic need: meaning in life. When there is a lack of meaning, you kill yourself because nothing matters and suffering which is in all of life, is pointless.[7] Viktor Frankl said a will to live which can endure suffering requires a *meaning to life*[8], a summon bonum. For life to be meaningful I believe that we need to know the importance of wisdom and virtue. Kreeft asks: Are our human objectives for living good and meaningful? Or is the play, plot, characters, and theme, pointless? Valueless?[9]

I will say along with Kreeft, that finite values such as materialism—don't put first. We need to ask: why be healthy? Why survive? What is the motive for survival? What for? If a person idolizes health, they will fail. But as Kreeft points out, our soul still cannot be our own last end. There has to be a good greater than the individual soul—which is God. Humans will only find perfect happiness in relation to God, our creator. In light of this, we are having a lover's quarrel with the world. Humans have unlimited desires which the world can't meet; we need an unlimited God to answer all our unlimited desires.[10]

Jesus tells us, or rather, *commands us*, to love our enemies and to turn the other cheek. The real, authentic manner of following Christ is to obey his words. *"Why do you call me 'Lord, Lord,' and not do what I tell you?"* Luke 6:46 (ESV). I have found that it is impossible for me to love my enemies without fervent prayer, asking the Lord to enable me to do this. *Oh, God, give me the strength to love my enemies. Fill me with forgiveness.* Without loving enemies, we have to cease attending church services, because churches are made up of imperfect human beings and some come across as belligerent. They often sit next to us on the pew. Their voices or looks attack and condemn. Why do the bullies sometimes seem more powerful in a church setting than the gentle, loving ones? Why do the bullies have so much power

6. Phil Cary, email to author, 3/29/2021.

7. Kreeft, *Ethics: History of Moral Thought,* audio CD.

8. Frankl, "Significance of Meaning for Health," 180.

9. Kreeft, *Ethics: History of Moral Thought,* audio CD.

10. Kreeft, *Ethics: History of Moral Thought,* audio CD.

in a church structure? Where is this God who claims in scripture that he will defend the poor, oppressed, and weak? Where is God in the church? *Lord, help me to love my enemies; they know not what they do. Help me to forgive the same way you have forgiven me of my trespasses.* Even Jesus had problems with the scribes and Pharisees, some leaders in the religious community. Jesus was opposed.

CS Lewis wrote in his allegory on heaven and hell, *The Great Divorce,* about people who quarrel and bicker with their neighbors, they don't like each other (and I would add, don't forgive), so they move to homes further away from each other. Then in the place they've moved to they don't like or forgive the neighbors there either, so they move even farther away. And on it goes, continuing until they keep moving farther and farther away from people, further and further out of town until the homes are all separated by millions of miles and distant galaxies.[11]

Nearing the end of this book I sense I must address the subject of pain. People with mental illness not only have to cope with on-going symptoms that can often lead to distress. They also have to find a way to survive the stigma confronting them on a day-to-day basis. Bullying, psychological and emotional mistreatment, is real. Those who have the privilege of being born with everything favorable for their success in this world are not aware of our hardships. We may cry out to God for help; but sometimes, it doesn't feel like God hears. I will compare this perpetual emotional pain with physical pain. I said to Phil Cary, "I'm kind of discouraged. I had a major surgery on my neck and for weeks I've prayed, asking God to heal me, specifically, to be healed from the severe pain because of the incision. I am incapacitated, and what godly use is that? I can't work on projects or do household chores. I feel as though my prayers for several weeks now are going unheard."

Phil Cary: The apostle speaks of suffering producing patience (or endurance, perseverance) which produces character, which produces hope, and hope is fulfilled by love. Rom. 5:3–5 (ESV). Unlike me, I figure, he speaks as one who knows. He's someone who's been through a lot of suffering, persecution and tribulation. Evidently there are things you can accomplish, and ways you can honor God, when that kind of patience (endurance or perseverance) has been formed in you. Perhaps patience opens the door to a kind of hard-won hope that those who suffer less don't experience. And I am certain that suffering draws you closer to Christ, one way or another.[12] For many people with chronic mental illness, *religion provides a powerful source of comfort and hope . . . Religious or spiritual interventions may help*

11. Lewis, *Great Divorce*, 9–11.
12. Phil Cary, email to author, 1/18/21.

[people with mental illness] utilize their spiritual resources to improve functioning, reduce isolation, and facilitate healing.[13]

When modern-day people are isolated in independent dwellings such as apartments or condos, this can cause emotional problems such as depression and anxiety. For good mental health, friends and relatives need to support these individuals, and maintain good contact in various ways such as with phones, (text or voice), emails, visits, and outings. Good mental health requires both a vertical connection with God and a horizontal connection with other people. Here we see the symbolism in the form of a cross. However, confusion sets in when we see what Christ says about close relatives. He stressed loyalty to him as something we should prioritize. For example, what does it mean when Christ says to not go back to say farewell to family when Christ calls us to follow him? Leaving the dead to bury their own dead? (Luke 9:60–62) What does Christ mean when he says to *hate* your spouse and family members? "If anyone comes to me and does not *hate* his own father and mother and wife and children and brothers and sisters, yes, and even his own life, he cannot be my disciple." Luke 14:26 (ESV) To give up everything? *Enemies are those in our own household?* Matt. 10:36 (ESV) How can we understand these passages when our heart leans toward loving our relatives and they start of occupy most of our free time? Does Christ mean that our first love is to be toward God, and then all else will be like hatred in comparison?

Here is one explanation from theologian Phil Cary: The basic framework here is not individual behavior or feelings, but the life of communities. The followers of Christ are a new social Body, and they call each other brothers and sisters—a new kind of family. That immediately makes their community, the church, a rival to the families we are all born into. And in the ancient world, that creates a huge upheaval. The ancient family is not just the modern nuclear family. It's an extended power structure, in many places much more powerful than the government, and it claims people. We in the modern West hardly know what that's like. What the NT calls *family* is more like what we might call a clan or even a tribe. If you read [Barack] Obama's memoir, *Dreams of My Father*, about his visit back to his distant kin in Africa, you might get a sense of it. His extended family, his clan, *claims* him, his future, his self, his resources. (One reason Africa does not do well in the global economy is because individual income tends to get absorbed and redistributed into the whole family, clan or tribe, so that you don't get capital accumulation and investment. You see that dynamic in Obama's memoir.)

13. Koenig, McCullough, Larson, *Religion and Health,* 165.

Christ defies this ancient power structure and says instead: *I* claim you, and this new clan of brothers and sisters claims you, and your resources, your wealth, your energy. These aspects of your life, your strengths, don't belong to your old clan any more, the clan which is yours by nature and by the flesh. This has immense practical consequences. When you get old and sick in the ancient world, it's the clan/family that takes care of you (because it would shame the clan/family if its members were seen to be beggars). Now, in the new clan, if you are old or sick or needy, it is no longer your blood relatives who care for you (they have probably rejected you because of your new allegiance). You depend on these new brothers and sisters, who are not your kin according to the flesh, but who share with you in the resurrected life of Jesus and in the hope of his coming. I think the application of these passages to the modern world means that the claim of Christ takes precedence over all other loyalties, no matter how scandalous that might be. In the modern world, that includes our professional and business lives, which are more identity-forming for most of us in our adulthood than our families. It means casting a suspicious eye on every form of security we think we have, including insurance, retirement accounts, and so on, which do the work that ancient family/clans did. You can actually see this play out in traumatized communities, both in inner–city America and in rural communities, where the church is one of the few institutions still intact, where people are treated like people rather than a case for some kind of bureaucrat or caseworker. Ironically, in light of the passages we're discussing, the church is one of the few places where families are supported rather than torn apart. (Often, in America government *help* undermines families). It's ironic, but not really surprising. In a modern culture where the family is already torn apart by social and economic forces (today this includes the opioid epidemic, which is making some people a lot of money), the church is the last fallback, because it is a place of loyalties that resist, however imperfectly, the imperatives of the capitalist market. I think that's the result of the kind of teaching you have in these passages. But to see that you have to step back from an individualistic reading (as if this is all about how you personally feel about your mother) and see what this is saying about the lives of [entire] communities.[14] [End of Phil Cary's comments on family.]

I, personally, need to point out that, in addition, when the physical family is destructive or perverted, i.e., the brothers harassing and sexually assaulting sisters (emotionally and/or physically), and fathers harassing or molesting children (emotionally and/or physically), then the physical family is no longer a source of support (financially or psychologically) for a

14. Phil Cary, email to author, 3/14/2019.

mentally ill person—both during childhood and later, as an adult. What usually happens then is that the federal and state governments with their social programs take the place of the physical family. However, the government will inevitably fail at some point which means that the church will have to provide a safety net. But a problem emerges when a single female (especially one who has been labeled with a mental illness diagnosis—either legitimately or not) joins a religious community where she hopes to form new, healthy church family relationships, there are some instances when a male in the religious community will mistreat and sexually harass the female church member, especially if she is single. I, personally, as a single woman serving in a church ministry, was sexually harassed by a male until he left the church. He seemed obsessed, was constantly staring at me, walking up to me with no respect for personal boundaries, and appeared to be lacking a conscience. When I shared with him my concern and discomfort and especially that I did not welcome his attention, he acknowledged his staring, saying, "I see the love of Christ in you." As an insensitive womanizer, he emotionally abused his spouse by openly seeking other women's attention and affection. I tried to avoid him as much as possible and was very relieved when he left my church. During this whole experience it made my church experience hell. The environment there during this time period was one of fighting off a predator when the church is supposed to be a safe place where one can find peace and healing.

Women still cannot seek justice in the church leadership hierarchy even in this day and age because it is still structured by males who want to silence females and keep women who speak out, "in their place." In addition, there are even Christian women who will not defend female victims of abuse and oppression, even in their own church. Knowing it was futile, in my silence I sought God as my refuge and knew that the ultimate vengeance comes not from myself, but from the Lord. *Beloved, never avenge yourselves, but leave it to the wrath of God, for it is written, "Vengeance is mine, I will repay, says the Lord."* Romans 12:19 (ESV) Until men and women purify their hearts and personally internalize Christ's righteous characteristics, obeying God's command, *You shalt not commit adultery*, Exodus 20:14 (ESV), people will not be safe anywhere—even in the church.

❖ ❖ ❖

As I close, in full retrospect of the battle, I see that the Lord gave me a mission along with many others in the past, present, and future, to assist in the liberation of the mentally ill. But in order to do that from a patient's perspective I had to experience such oppression myself. And coming from out of the turmoil and affliction I emerged into a person that came to know God as her savior and Jesus as Lord. To illustrate my sense of mission, I want to share with you what happened one day before I gave a presentation at the start of my ministry.

When I began my Mental Health Initiatives (MHI) ministry many years ago, my primary focus along with writing, was to present the ideas in PowerPoint presentations, at first, given by invitation to groups. I remember on the morning of one of the first talks for a senior group at St. Andrew Presbyterian Church as I got ready to go, I felt great stress and anguish because I knew the gravity of the situation and importance for getting MHI off the ground as someone in recovery and an advocate for the mentally ill. The information I was to present dealt with the tragic history of psychiatric care in my area and the suffering of those mentally ill who had been put away at the rudimentary facility at the Johnson County Poor Farm in the 1860s. And then I provided more information up to the present day. Creation of the sides and narrative took almost eight months of focused, tedious labor. This work of presentation for this church group that day extracted much psychic and emotional energy from my being as I grasped the gravity of the situation, and I was in severe distress.

That morning, as I struggled to get ready to go out, dressing, fixing my hair, I looked at myself in the mirror and saw small spots of blood on the skin of my face. I learned later that this was hematidrosis, or hematohidrosis. It is a very rare medical condition that causes you to ooze or sweat blood from your skin when you're not cut or injured. It usually happens on or around the face. Sometimes it seems to be caused by extreme [emotional] distress or fear, such as facing death, torture, or severe ongoing abuse. It's probably where the term "sweating blood," meaning a great effort, comes from. Only a few handfuls of hematidrosis cases were confirmed in medical studies in the 20th century. Doctors don't know exactly what triggers hematidrosis, in part because it's so rare. They think it could be related to your body's "fight or flight" response.[15] In a way I was experiencing carrying a cross like the Lord Jesus who was sweating blood before the crucifixion when praying:

And [Jesus Christ] came out and went, as was his custom, to the Mount of Olives, and the disciples followed him. And when he came to the place, he said to them, "Pray that you may not enter into temptation." And he withdrew from them about a stone's throw, and knelt down and prayed, saying, "Father, if you are willing, remove this cup from me. Nevertheless, not my will, but yours, be done." And there appeared to him an angel from heaven, strengthening him. And being in agony he prayed more earnestly;

15. WebMD, "What is Hematidrosis," para 2–4, 8.

and his sweat became like great drops of blood falling down to the ground. Luke 22:39–44 (ESV).

I am reminded of this verse: But I do not account my life of any value nor as precious to myself, if only I may finish my course and the ministry that I received from the Lord Jesus, to testify to the gospel of the grace of God. Acts 20:24 (ESV)

However, in all honesty, can I really say I've achieved the *abundant life*? As I write, the day after a national holiday, I have been reminded that when all connections are gone for me except the internet, what life do I really have? When public transportation, i.e., buses, are not in operation, cabs are too expensive, and I have no vehicle of my own, how can I go out to be around other human beings of like interests? I have to use two crutches to go anywhere, so walking many city blocks is not realistic and is embarrassing. Therapists and doctors are off work, all the pools are closed, the churches are closed, libraries are closed. Almost all friends are busy with family and have no time or desire to visit me at my home. My physical family is out to lunch, as they have been my entire life. I find that I am still the outcast, still isolated, and without purpose—on holidays. And when I am socially excluded in this manner, life loses all meaning and I literally cannot function. Even academia has done research on this very topic. In *Alone and Without Purpose: Life Loses Meaning Following Social Exclusion*, social psychologists ask:

> Where do people find meaning in life? In principle, people could find meaning in communing with nature or with divinity, engaging in philosophical or religious contemplation, pursuing scientific or artistic or technological innovation, or other potentially solitary pursuits. Life's meaning does not obviously or inherently depend on social relations. Yet in practice, it seems likely that people find meaning in their social relations. Unlike most other animals, humans obtain much of what they need from their social group, rather than directly from the natural environment.[16]

On holidays, I am cut off from the things that give me meaning. Except for an out of state advisor who will converse in some brief, but valuable, email discussions, or a few minutes of phone conversation with a couple of neighbors or a brief text, my usual supports are gone: The public and university libraries where I do research and read and write, along with the kind librarians who assist me. I am unable to go to coffee shops to be with the companions (yet strangers) who frequent them; the pools are closed where

16. Stillman et al., "Alone and Without Purpose," para 2.

I receive a friendly greeting; and polite church people who occasionally interact with me—all of these things are not available on a holiday. And as a result, I feel lost, and can do little at home where it seems like a dark cloud has come over me and I am drowning in sea of meaninglessness. *The belief that one is living a meaningful life is associated with positive functioning.*[17] I become immobile and take to my bed, in the dark, waiting and praying for the next day when I will be set free from my apartment and isolation, and, yes, the humiliation. The humiliation of those rejected, excluded, and abandoned.

So, no, there has not been a full or completed integration into the Christian community, at least, not yet. It will take more time. Our brothers and sisters in Christ still stay aloof, at least on these few holidays a year. They are busy with their own lives and families, and so, my spiritual home, really, is with other rejected human beings wherever they are in the society, others who are marginalized and isolated. There is this *invisible bond of isolation* which is paradoxical in, and of, itself. I write this book for you and say that our hope is in God and, in God, alone.

Glory to God.

---

17. Stillman et al., "Alone and Without Purpose," para 4.

Appendix A

What is a Virtue?

By Phillip Cary, Prof. of Philosophy, Eastern University

WHAT *KIND* OF THING IS A VIRTUE?

- A *habit* or disposition or *shape* of the soul, like a skill.
- Like all habits, we have it even when not using it (e.g., when sleeping). A courageous man has the virtue of courage even when not doing courageous deeds, just as a pianist is still a pianist (has the skill of piano playing) even in her sleep.
- Like skill, virtue is an *intelligent* habit, not merely mechanical. It is connected with how accurately we perceive the world, and thus it cannot exist without wisdom. (Good intentions without wisdom are not virtues).
- You can think of a virtue as *the form or shape of a soul*, the way a well-exercised body is in better shape than an unhealthy body. Also, shape or form always means boundaries: an honest person's soul has boundaries it will not cross.
- This shaping of the soul is why we speak of Christian *formation*.

WHAT KIND OF HABIT?

- A *good habit*. Like skill, virtue is always about doing things *well*. Because doing things well is how we accomplish things, a virtue is also a kind of power.

- A *difficult habit*. We cannot learn to do things well without effort. Virtuous actions are difficult, as Aristotle explains, because "It is easy to miss the target, hard to hit it."

- A *pleasant habit*. A virtuous person takes pleasure in virtuous actions for their own sake (much like a skilled person who enjoys exercising her skill). A virtuous person sees moral behavior as worthwhile for its own sake, not just for its good results.

- A *habit of action*: courage is a tendency to act courageously, kindness is a tendency to act kindly, etc. Like a skill, a virtue makes doing the appropriate actions easier.

- A *habit of perception*. E.g., courageous people see the world differently than cowards: they see threats as something to fight, not run away from, etc.

- A *habit of feeling*. E.g., a kind person is moved to compassion rather than being indifferent to the suffering of others.

- A *habit of thought*. For all these reasons, a virtuous person thinks about the world differently than a vicious person does.

CLASSICAL VIRTUES (ACQUIRED BY PRACTICE)

- *Courage*: the habit of dealing well with pain and danger.
- *Temperance*: the habit of dealing well with pleasure and enticement.
- *Justice*: rendering to everyone what they deserve or are owed ("to each his due").
- *Prudence*: practical moral wisdom, knowing how to do the right thing.

CHRISTIAN VIRTUES (RECEIVED AS GIFTS, BUT STRENGTHENED BY PRACTICE)

Faith, hope and love (1 Cor. 13)

- *Faith* is formed in our hearts not by practice (i.e., by works!) but by the Word of Christ which is impressed on our hearts by the Holy Spirit.

- *Hope and Love* follow from Faith: Through faith we are joined to Christ by the power of the Holy Spirit to please the Father, and therefore believers gladly follow Christ and obey God (i.e., by loving him with whole heart and neighbor as themselves) thus bearing the fruit of the Spirit, including hope.

Appendix B

A Question of Education

Scott R. Grau
Adjunct Instructor of History
Kirkwood Community College, Iowa City Branch
July 30, 2021

Author Marcia Murphy asks in her introduction how mental integrity is to be achieved in light of serious mental illness. As a person with no background in either psychology or psychiatry, that is not a question on which I am prepared even to offer an opinion, much less suggest an answer. However, in her efforts to explore this issue, she does raise some interesting and important issues of learning, education, and the question of how we think.

As someone who has spent some time teaching, I have thought a lot about learning and education in general, and more fundamentally, intellectual integrity, which, I think, is related to mental integrity. That, it seems to me, is of concern to anyone and everyone who spends time thinking about thinking.

Clearly there are many kinds of learning, many very different kinds of intelligence, and no single method, theory, or system of education that can answer for them all. It seems to me that the purpose of any education is to bring out and develop capabilities and aptitudes that are otherwise latent and undeveloped. Moreover, in learning about other things, practices, and ideas, one can come to a better understanding of oneself. This means, at least in part, challenging the learner to expand and grow in areas of understanding and capability that otherwise might remain as unrealized potential.

Education, at least for me, also means an openness to the world, coming prepared with a curiosity and a sense of adventure to expand horizons, explore new perspectives, and engage with an always complex reality in both old ways and new. A proper education offers us the opportunity to move beyond our narrowly circumscribed reality to investigate and discover new things, old things, people and places we know, and people, places, and ideas we have never known. And, in coming to understand these things, we can come to a better understanding of ourselves and our place in the world, and indeed, the universe.

This all requires a powerful degree of intellectual honesty and courage, the willingness to sometimes get things wrong, and humility in the understanding of how little we really do know. Yet at the same time, it is important to develop and gain the confidence that with work and perseverance we can push back the limits of our own ignorance; in doing this, develop our own minds, abilities, and the capacity for questioning as a means of gaining a new and better understanding of our world.

Appendix C

A Reflection on Stewardship

Essay Written by Russell Noyes Jr., MD

Originally published in newsletter of Christ the King Lutheran Church, Iowa City, Iowa, 2000

WHEN I WAS A senior medical student, God called me to become a psychiatrist. At the time, I could not have said what attracted me to the field, but looking back, I think I was drawn to the mystery and intellectual challenge it presented. In addition, I recognized in myself a feeling for mentally ill people that could be important in understanding and working with them. Then too, I saw that they were often demoralized if not stigmatized and that for them I could be an advocate.

When Jesus asked the man at Bethesda if he wished to be healed, he replied, "Sir, I have no man to put me into the pool when the water is troubled, and while I am going, another steps down before me" (John 5:7). His words convey the alienation and helpless resignation often experienced by those with severe mental disorders. Many, in addition to illness, face overwhelming circumstances, and like the lepers of Jesus' day, know the disapproval of their families and communities. But, the mentally ill of this world are part of God's creation. They are children of God, created in His image, and mindful of this, I strive to show them the respect and concern they are due. If healing occurs, it is by the grace of God. Medication and therapy are His instruments.

I have been fortunate to see great progress in the field of psychiatry over my 40-year career. Effective treatments have been developed for what were once thought to be untreatable conditions. This has meant that lives have been changed and the stigma attached to illness has lessened. I thank God for the opportunity he has given me to witness and share in these advances. I am also grateful for the opportunity I have had to serve these people in need. Through the years I have gained increasing respect for those who struggle with mental illness. Their view of the world enriches us and their courage gives us strength. And, their faith in the face of hardship glorifies God.

Appendix D

Resources on the Reality
of Spiritual Conflict

BOOKS

Amorth, Fr. Gabriele, *An Exorcist Explains the Demonic: The Antics of Satan and His Army of Fallen Angels.* Translated by Charlotte J. Fasi.. Manchester: Sophia Institute, 2016.

Martin, Malachi. *Hostage to the Devil: The Possession and Exorcism of Five Contemporary Americans.* San Francisco: Harper, 1976,1992.

Allen, Thomas B. *Possessed,* Lincoln, NE: iUniverse, 1994, 2000

Murphy, Ed. The Handbook for Spiritual Warfare, 3rd Ed: Nashville: Thomas Nelson, 2003.

Prince, Derek. *They Shall Expel Demons: What You Need to Know about Demons—Your Invisible Enemies.* Grand Rapids: Chosen Books at Baker, 1998.

Murphy, Marcia A. *Voices in the Rain: Meaning in Psychosis.* Eugene: Wipf and Stock, 2018.

The Holy Bible

ARTICLES

Murphy, Marcia A. "[Coping With] The Spiritual Meaning of Psychosis." *Psychiatric Rehabilitation Journal* 24, no. 2, (2000) 179–183. https://hopeforrecovery.com/coping-spiritual-meaning-psychosis/

Murphy, Marcia A. "Psychiatric Illness from the Religious Perspective." Mental Health Initiatives (1997). https://hopeforrecovery.com/psychiatric-illness-religious-perspective/

Bibliography

Adeney-Risakotta, Bernard T. *Living in a Sacred Cosmos: Indonesia and the Future of Islam*. New Haven: Yale University Southeast Asia Studies, 2018.

Allen, Thomas B. *Possessed,* Lincoln: iUniverse, 1994, 2000.

Amen, Daniel, G. *The End of Mental Illness: How Neuroscience Is Transforming Psychiatry and Helping Prevent or Reverse Mood and Anxiety Disorders, ADHD, Addictions, PTSD, Psychosis, Personality Disorders, and More.* Carol Stream: Tyndale Momentum, 2020.

American Psychiatric Association. "Psychiatrists." *Diagnostic and Statistical Manual of Mental Disorders (DSM-5)*. https://www.psychiatry.org/psychiatrists/practice/dsm

American Psychological Association. *Diagnostic and Statistical Manual of Disorders, Fifth Edition*. Arlington: American Psychological Association, 2013.

Amorth, Fr. Gabriele, *An Exorcist Explains the Demonic: The Antics of Satan and His Army of Fallen Angels*. Translated by Charlotte J. Fasi.. Manchester: Sophia Institute, 2016.

Boisen, Anton T. *The Exploration of the Inner World: A Study of Mental Disorder and Religious Experience*. New York: Harper and Brothers, 1936.

Borba, Michele. *End Peer Cruelty, Build Empathy*. Minneapolis: Free Spirit, 2018.

Carlson, Erica W. *Understanding the Quantum World*. DVD. Chantilly: Teaching Company, 2019.

Cary, Phillip, "The Classic View." In *God and the Problem of Evil: Five Views*, edited by Chad Meister and James K. Dew Jr., 13–36. Downers Grove: InterVarsity Press Academic, 2017.

———*The Meaning of Protestant Theology: Luther, Augustine, and the Gospel that Gives Us Christ*. Grand Rapids: Baker Academic, 2019.

Clarken, Rodney H., "Moral Intelligence in the Schools." Paper presented at the Annual Meeting of the Michigan Academy of Sciences, Arts and Letters. Detroit: Mar 20, 2009.

Dillard, Annie. *Teaching a Stone to Talk: Expeditions and Encounters*. New York: Harper & Row, 1982.

Donelson, Earle. "The Importance of Values and Morals." *Lifelines: Exploring Life Issues*. accessed 10/12/2021. http://www.explorefaith.org/lifelines_morals.html

Donne, John. *Devotions upon Emergent Occasions*. Cambridge: The University Press, 1923.

Duquesne University. *Pygmalion Effect*. https://www.duq.edu/about/centers-and-institutes/center-for-teaching-excellence/teaching-and-learning-at-duquesne/pygmalion

Frankl, Viktor. "The Significance of Meaning for Health" in *Religion and Medicine: Essays on Meaning, Values, and Health,* edited by David Belgum, 177–185. Ames: Iowa State University Press, 1967.

Fraser, Giles. The Guardian, "Nietzsche's Passionate Atheism was the Making of Me." 2/05/2012. https://www.theguardian.com/commentisfree/2012/feb/05/passionate-atheism-me-christianity-nietzsche#:~:text=It%20isn't%20a%20eureka,God%20walked%20into%20the%20restaurant.

Greyson, Bruce. *After, A Doctor Explores What Near-Death Experiences Reveal about Life and Beyond.* New York: St. Martin's Essentials, 2021.

Information Philosopher, "Eugene Wigner." accessed 10/12/2021. https://www.informationphilosopher.com/solutions/scientists/wigner/#:~:text=Eugene%20Wigner%20made%20quantum%20physics,ever%20happens%20in%20the%20universe

James, William. *The Varieties of Religious Experience: A Study in Human Nature.* New York: Modern Library, 1902.

Kellehear, Allan. *Experiences Near Death: Beyond Medicine and Religion.* Oxford: Oxford University Press, 1996.

Keller, Timothy J. *Counterfeit Gods: The Empty Promises of Money, Sex, and Power, and the Only Hope That Matters.* New York: Dutton, 2009.

———"Hope Beyond the Walls of the World," HKU, presentation, video, 4/05/14.

———*The Reason for God: Belief in an Age of Skepticism.* New York: Penguin, 2008, 2018.

Kelsey, Morton T. *Encounter with God.* Minneapolis: Bethany Fellowship, 1972.

———*The Other Side of Silence: A Guide to Christian Meditation.* New York: Paulist, 1976.

———*The Reality of the Spiritual World.* Pecos, New Mexico: Dove, 1974.

Kierkegaard, Soren Aabye. *The Sickness Unto Death: A Christian Psychological Exposition for Upbuilding and Awakening.* Translated by Walter Lowrie. Princeton: Princeton University Press, 1941.

Kinsella, M. T., and C. Monk. "Impact of Maternal Stress, Depression and Anxiety on Fetal Neurobehavioral Development." *Clinical Obstetrics and Gynecology* 52, no. 3 Sep 2009. 425–40. accessed on 10/12/2021. https://doi.org/10.1097/GRF.0b013e3181b52df1

Koenig, Harold G., and Michael E McCullough, David B. Larson, eds. *Handbook of Religion and Health.* Oxford University Press, 2001.

Kreeft, Peter. *Ethics: A History of Moral Thought.* Audio CD. Recorded Books, LLC, 2004.

Laino, Charlene, "Brain Exercises May Delay Memory Loss: Study Shows Activities Like Reading Magazines Are Linked to Lower Risk of Dementia." WebMD, 4/29/2009. accessed on 8/16/202. https://www.webmd.com/brain/news/20090429/brain-exercises-may-delay-memory-loss

Leas, Robert. *The Biography of Anton Theophilus Boisen.* Association for Clinical Pastoral Education, Inc. https://www.acpe.edu/pdf/History/The%20Biography%20of%20Anton%20Theophilus%20Boisen.pdf

Lewis, C.S. *The Great Divorce: A Dream.* San Francisco: Harper, 2001.

———*Mere Christianity*, audio recording originally broadcast BBC radio, March, 21, 1944. YouTube: Apologetics 315, June 6, 2012.

Luhrmann, T.M. and Jocelyn Marrow, eds. *Our Most Troubling Madness: Case Studies in Schizophrenia Across Cultures*. Oakland: University of California Press, 2016.

Martin, Malachi. *Hostage to the Devil: The Possession and Exorcism of Five Contemporary Americans*. San Francisco: Harper, 1976,1992.

Mayo Clinic Staff. *Transcranial Magnetic Stimulation*. https://www.mayoclinic.org/tests-procedures/transcranial-magnetic-stimulation/about/pac-20384625

McDonald, William. "Kierkegaard's Life," Soren Kierkegaard. Stanford Encyclopedia of Philosophy, 2017. https://plato.stanford.edu/entries/kierkegaard/#Life page

Monaco, Kristen. *NDMA Prompts Metformin Recall: FDA finds certain products with excessive levels of potential carcinogen*. Medpage Today. 5/29/2020. https://www.medpagetoday.com/primarycare/diabetes/86757

Murphy, Ed. The Handbook for Spiritual Warfare, 3rd Ed: Nashville: Thomas Nelson, 2003.

Murphy, Marcia A. "[Coping With] The Spiritual Meaning of Psychosis." *Psychiatric Rehabilitation Journal* 24, no. 2, (2000) 179–183. https://hopeforrecovery.com/coping-spiritual-meaning-psychosis/

———"Psychiatric Illness from the Religious Perspective." Mental Health Initiatives (1997). https://hopeforrecovery.com/psychiatric-illness-religious-perspective/

———*Voices in the Rain: Meaning in Psychosis*. Eugene: Wipf & Stock, 2018.

New World Encyclopedia, "Friedrich Nietzsche: His Mental Breakdown." https://www.newworldencyclopedia.org/entry/Friedrich_Nietzsche#Credits

Peterson, Christopher, and Martin E. P. Seligman. *Character Strengths and Virtues: A Handbook and Classification*. Washington, DC: American Psychological Association, 2004.

Prince, Derek. *They Shall Expel Demons: What You Need to Know about* Demons—*Your Invisible Enemies*. Grand Rapids: Chosen Books at Baker, 1998.

Rhem, James. "Pygmalion in the Classroom." *The National Teaching & Learning Forum*. 8, no. 2 (1999) 1–2.

Shorter, Edward. *A History of Psychiatry: From the Era of the Asylum to the Age of Prozac*. New York: John Wiley & Sons, 1997.

Shtasel, Derri, et al. "Community Psychiatry: What Should Future Psychiatrists Learn?" *Harvard Review of Psychiatry*. Nov-Dec. 2012, 20 (6) 318–23. accessed on 10/12/2021. https://pubmed.ncbi.nlm.nih.gov/23216069/

Social Security Administration, Supplemental Security Income Program Description and Legislative History. accessed 9/28/2021. https://www.ssa.gov/policy/docs/statcomps/supplement/2012/ssi.html

Solzhenitsyn, Alexandr. "A World Split Apart." Commencement Address, Harvard University. June 8, 1978. American Rhetoric Online Speech Bank. accessed on 10/12/2021. https://www.americanrhetoric.com/speeches/alexandersolzhenitsyn harvard.htm

Stillman, Tyler F. et al. "Alone and Without Purpose: Life Loses Meaning Following Social Exclusion." *Journal of Experimental Social Psychology*. July 45, no.4 (2009) 686–694.

Vercillo, Kathryn. "10 Most Important Health Benefits of Yarncrafting." Lion Brand Notebook, 5/20/2014. accessed on 8/16/2021. http://blog.lionbrand.com/10-most-important-health-benefits-of-yarncrafting/.

Walters, Orville S. "Religion and Psychopathology." In *Religion and Medicine, Essays on Meaning, Values, and Health,* edited by David Belgum. Ames: Iowa State University Press, 119–134.

Wood, W. Jay. *Epistemology: Becoming Intellectually Virtuous.* Downers Grove: InterVarsity Press Academic, 1998.

Zidny, Robby and Ingo Eilks. "Integrating Perspectives from Indigenous Knowledge and Western Science in Secondary and Higher Chemistry Learning to Contribute to Sustainability Education." *Sustainable Chemistry and Pharmacy* 16 (2020) 1.